✓ 1st do not
✓ Always be

Divine Reflections

Receiving the Real Meaning
Of Hidden Messages

by

Michele Novak Stemmer

*To John,
Have a wonderful,
spiritual journey!
Michele Novak Stemmer*

ISBN-10 - 1482713934

Dedication

This book is dedicated to everyone on earth who has major challenges in their lives hoping to find the real or spiritual reason why this misfortune has come their way.

CONTENTS

Chapter VIII - Mother Nature

Chapter IX - Messages

Conclusion

Foreword

Upon reviewing Divine Reflections, we learn the value of observing what appears at first glance to be coincidences are actually pieces of the puzzle about our journey here on earth.

Michele Novak Stemmer introduces how each experience is colorfully woven into the fabric of this lifetime as divine reflections abound. She recalls her personal revelations through predictions, premonitions, names, numbers, signs and symbols -- and most significantly, divine guidance.

Our lives are important and meaningful in every moment. We are here to embrace each other in fellowship and love, treat with respect to the Source and the sacred principles of life.

Michele's collective experiences and reflections serve as a reminder that there are no accidents, only our free will and divine intervention ... guiding us to achieve our highest potential.

Reverend Grace

Acknowledgments

With much gratitude and love:

To my dear departed father for his true devotion and assistance in dealing with difficult situations in my life. I know his watchful eye is still looking over me from heaven. I'll always remember his words ''Keep your chin up''.

To my wonderful mother who has left the earth. She used to say that we often exchange one set of problems for another set of problems. I am very grateful that she was easy going and always took a special interest in me.

To my terrific son Michael and daughter-in-law Theresa for providing their help at a moment's notice and being there through many challenging situations.

To my wonderful son Marc and daughter-in-law Laurel for all the time they have spent visiting me and the help and support they have provided to make my life run smoothly. A special thank you goes to Laurel for her tireless effort with chores, shopping, cooking, etc.

To my precious granddaughter Jennifer Lynn who brings so much happiness into my life. Her sweet smile makes my heart so joyous.

To my dear sister Diane and best friend Suzanne. I truly appreciate all the advice and kindness they have given me through the years.

To my good friend Patricia for her continued support. Also, I'm very grateful for all her suggestions and assistance in editing this book to make my dream come true.

To my helpers Cameron and Peggy who assist me in the kitchen. They also take me to appointments, the store, and social events, etc.

A special thank you to Rebecca Sherwood for helping me make this book possible. I truly appreciate all her advice and support on this journey that brings a special message to all.

To some of my health practitioners Robert Lewanski, Health Force center Dr. Cody, Jackie Featherley, Micki Jones, Carol Lechko and my Young Living consultant Marlene Wiegers for their recommendations which have improved my health.

Introduction

The most important thing in life is to have a strong belief in God or Source. Secondly, we must be aware of the world around us. We know that this whole Universe including Jesus, the heavenly angels, saints, and your guides are right there to help you every step of the way.

To get in touch with these powers, God, through the Holy Spirit, helps when we seek the truth. Sometimes we are troubled in our lives and complain and often blame each other. But every time we suffer, there is a lesson to be learned. If we don't learn the lesson the first time, it will repeat until we get it right. As humans we are all co-creators with God. I believe we are destined to fulfill God's divine plan for us here on earth. Life is like many small puzzle pieces that fit together to form a big picture.

I am a very spiritual person with a heartfelt commitment to share with everyone that there is a bright side to every negative situation. Looking at life's experiences through a higher awareness has brought me to levels of understanding that I never knew were possible. This has kept me afloat while sailing through the rough seas of life.

I encourage everyone to stop, look, and listen to the clues in their lives. Also, by keeping a daily journal of each event, these clues will have special meanings.

1. Something good comes from something bad. There are no bad experiences.

2. All things happen for a reason.

3. Events fall into place at the right time and place. We must detach ourselves from the outcome we desire. If it doesn't happen soon, be assured the Universe will bring it about at the right time.

4. There are no such things as coincidences- everything happens in divine order. When we are truly awake, we will see hidden messages from spirit through chance encounters, unusual events, accidents, etc.

5. When we ask or pray for help, answers will come to us through a friend, a book, a radio show, television, etc.

6. We must set an intention each day by stating how we want our day to unfold to bring us happiness and strength to carry out our mission.

Spiritually, we can receive what we ask for quickly by living pure spirit. This allows us into the state of the miraculous where God or Source brings us miracles at the exact time we need them. Also, it is such a comfort to know that we are never given more than we can handle.

It's important to remember that every physical event has a spiritual cause. The spiritual meaning is the real meaning for everything. We must not let the ego stand in our way even though it tries to control us.

We are now on this earth plane, but many planes of existence are available to us. When we transition from earth, our real home is on another spiritual plane which is determined by our soul's progression.

A few stories written in this book happened many years ago. The information of what had transpired from that time on is accurate because I have kept a daily journal since 1992. Also, the data presented regarding historical events, dates, etc. was thoroughly researched and is true to the best of my knowledge.

This book has a collection of stories that stand on their own so that you, the reader, can read each story separately if you choose. Please note that there is some repetition of names and places, but they all have a common thread of living a spiritual life.

Chapter I

Major Events

Liberty Life Insurance Company in 1998

The Titanic Connection

I have always been fascinated throughout my adult life with the possibility that when the physical body leaves the earth, our soul continues to exist and will inhabit many bodies over the course of time. So when my son Marc and I moved to Greenville, South Carolina for sixteen months in February of 1998, I felt that the spiritual reason I moved was to bring me in direct contact with the causal plane of existence-- the plane where past lives are stored.

My life became quite challenging as a single mother of two boys since my divorce four years prior. Marc was upset about his high school classes starting at 7:30 a.m. so he researched the circadian rhythms of teenagers. Most high school students sleep forty minutes less on school nights, so they lose their concentration and tend to doze off during class. In light of this, Marc asked me if we could move to a school in the South where classes began later.

Greenville was a beautiful city with breathtaking scenery including huge waterfalls and sparkling streams flowing throughout the mountainous areas. It's no wonder that they had chosen this location to film the movie "Last of the Mohicans" years ago.

We lived at the Chimney's Apartments in the city of Taylors for about five months. We then had to move to the Oak Ridge Apartments in Greenville to be in the proper school district so Marc could attend Riverside High School. He was fortunate enough to attend one of the top high schools in the state. During his tenure at Riverside, he was an enthusiastic participant in his speech class; and I loved judging the speech competitions. He also enjoyed being on the track team.

I wanted to keep working steadily and enjoy diversified assignments, so I registered with five temporary agencies. My assignments included working for a dentist, an attorney, an evening telemarketing position, among others.

My first assignment while at Liberty Life Insurance Company was in the Call Center. Like a waking dream, this building bore a strong resemblance to a ship. My second assignment was on the lower level in the mailroom at the rear of that building. I could hear loud machine noises, like those from a ship's engine, while a sound from machinery in the adjoining room reminded me of a boat horn. It seemed peculiar, and a fellow co-worker agreed.

One day, while peering out the mailroom's window I saw a three-sided deck, surrounded by a metal railing, reminding me of a ship's deck. Intrigued, I visited the local library and checked out an illustrated book about the RMS Titanic.

My third assignment was located at Liberty Direct as a receptionist in the front office (or what I perceived as the bow of a ship). While sitting at my desk, I felt that I was on a ship which encompassed my being. The ceiling was low and large windows covering the wall gave the illusion of openness...all that was missing was the ocean. Plus, the large pillars were similar to the ones on the Titanic. When leaving work one evening, as I walked down the hallway, it felt like I was on a boat deck because the hallway was curved, with windows on the entire outer wall. In the main lobby there was a huge staircase similar to the one on the Titanic, although less ornate. Both the Titanic and this building had a gymnasium.

As I walked out to my car, I observed that the exterior of Liberty Life was an architectural masterpiece. The front of the building was shaped into a point, similar to the stern of a large ship's bow.

Liberty Life Insurance Company's address was 2000 Wade Hampton, Greenville, South Carolina. One can see the two words South Hampton. This corresponds to Southampton, England where the ship began its journey on its way to New York. Also noticeable are the words lifeboat and steamship in the name and address.

The next day, while walking down the first floor hallway, I noticed the wall hangings had XXX designs which were identical to those on the Titanic's furniture and decorations. Also, sounds of a boat engine were clearly heard.

When I left work that day, an eerie feeling came over me-- that I was once on a ship, possibly the Titanic. Could I be reliving a past life? I then began to think of this as a large puzzle; with each piece representing information that supports my connection.

To begin, the name of Liberty Life past President is Hayne Hipp--add an S to Hipp and see the word ship. The name of Liberty Life past Executive Vice President John Smith is the same as the captain of the Titanic Edward John Smith. Speaking of similar names, Fred Remer, my former boss in Michigan reminded me of Fremer. Fremer is a French Oceanographic Institute which excavated parts of the Titanic wreck site in 1987, where some 800 artifacts were brought up.

In addition, John Jacob Astor was age 47 when he was killed by a falling smokestack on the ship's bridge as the Titanic sank. His wife, Madeleine was also 47 when she lost her life from heart disease on 3-27-1940. (My birthdate of 10-7-1949 is in that date). At my former residence in Michigan, 4799 Berkshire, we see 47- the age of the Astors at the time of their demise. If we compare 3-27-1940 to 4799 we find the numbers have 479 in common. I lived in Building 22 at my condo. The Titanic sank at 2:20 a.m. on April 15, 1912. Their son, John Jacob Astor VI passed away on June 26, 1992 at age 79. Number 79 is in 4799.

Life is full of miracles; so the following seems to suggest the possibility that I am Madeleine Force Astor reincarnated:

1. When Madeleine was pregnant on the ship, she wore button-down tunic tops. I also had three summer outfits with button-down tunic tops that resembled maternitywear. We both often wore identical head-bands.

2. John Jacob Astor, her husband, was the wealthiest man aboard the Titanic, with a net worth of 87 million dollars. He was 47 and she was 18 when they married; he being 29 years her senior. I too, have been attracted to older men since my divorce. Plus, when I went for an appraisal on my gold necklace, the salesman tried to sell me a diamond wedding ring- another symbol of marriage.

3. I worked for Future Force Temporary Agency in Michigan. 'Force' was Madeleine's maiden name.

4. My good friend, Liz Leslie's granddaughter's name is Madeline. My deceased friend Marie's middle name was Madeline, and my niece, Lisa, named her doll Madeleine. Also, when I looked inside one of her children's books, the name Ava appeared which was John Astor's ex-wife's name.

5. Madeleine Force Astor was put on lifeboat number 4. My life path is number 4 in numerology.

6. Madeleine and John Jacob Astor IV married on September 9, 1911. My goddaughter Erika was married on September 9. They honeymooned in Egypt and France; and were returning to America aboard the Titanic. Interestingly, one of my assignments was at Honeymoon Paper Products. The movie "The Prince of Egypt" was playing in Greenville, the library featured an Egyptian poster and the health food store had a paper pyramid...all reminders of Egypt.

7. They had only been married for seven months, and she was pregnant with his child when this steamship sank in the Atlantic Ocean. Their son John Jacob Astor VI

came into this world on August 14, 1912. We both had a son born under the astrological sign of Leo.

8. A well-known psychic medium said my daughter-in-law, Laurel, in a past life was Rosadile Bidois, a maid to Madeleine on the Titanic (Laurel often helps me now on a regular basis with house chores). Also, Caroline Louise Endres was Astor's private nurse. 'Louise' is my Confirmation name.

As for our second apartment, Oak Ridge, we chose to live on the second floor because a beautiful wooded area was visible next to our terrace. When looking out of the window of the apartment, the roof of another apartment resembled a pyramid. As we recall, the Astors honeymooned in France and Egypt. Our address was 150 Oak Ridge Place, No.15-P, Greenville, South Carolina 29615. Please note there are three 15's in the address. With close attention to details, 15 is important as it also relates to the Titanic which sank on April 15, 1912.

While touring this new apartment, we uncovered features that would relate to this ocean liner. The design on the white closet door and on the front door bore a striking resemblance to the design on the wall found in the ship's gymnasium. Our apartment balcony was the only one in the complex that had a lattice fence. The lattice fence matches the one found in Cafe Parisian, a restaurant on the Titanic. My television set's crisscross design is the same as that found in the ship's library. I have had this television set for nearly 20 years, never paying attention to the crisscross design.

Another magical event happened while still living in Greenville. A piece of mail addressed to my son, Michael, who was living in my house in Michigan, was delivered to me by mistake (or was it a mistake?) On the envelope appeared from "Titan Indemnity Company." The word Titanic is found in those three words.

Amongst my other mail was a telephone bill from Bell South with an advertisement inside the envelope with the word "Star." The Titanic belonged to White Star Lines.

Speaking of star, I have seen that word on the street signs, billboards, building signs, and have seen White Star Lines on trucks. Also, I had gone on a cruise ship years ago called "The Bahama Star".

When my parents and I dined at a Michigan restaurant, I noticed the jukebox song titled "A Night to Remember," which is also the title of a movie about the Titanic and the song "Star" listed together.

When I had worked as a telemarketer for Nationwide Insurance Company, I spoke to a lady on the phone whose last name was "Moody". Amazingly, the man in the crow's nest on the Titanic was Sixth Officer, James Moody.

He was one of the men that shouted "Iceberg ahead!" He had no binoculars so when the iceberg became visible, the ship could not change its course enough to avoid hitting the iceberg on the starboard hull.

Another person in my life, Gregory Semeroz, whom I've known since high school, could have possibly been on the Titanic with me. Like my friend, the leading stoker named Gregory was unmarried. My friend, Gregory, lived in Clinton Township. Obvious words in his address are "ton" meaning the poundage of a ship and "ship" relates to an ocean liner, in this example.

To fit in more of the puzzle pieces, I was reminded about the Titanic's hull when I speak of Lake Woodhull in Waterford, Michigan. This is where my sister, Diane, her husband, Jack, my niece, Lisa, and husband Jim and daughters Brooke and Kristina live; and where my deceased parents and grandmother used to live.

I really enjoyed gazing out of my bedroom window at my parents' home, to see the top of our boathouse deck. The deck had metal railings like the bow of a large boat--how I used to love to relax and sunbathe on this deck. I had read that the Astors were last seen as a couple on the deck. Also, when I went to the Titanic exhibit in Dearborn, Michigan, I noticed a wrought iron two-seated bench that truly resonated with me as well as seeing my neighbor's wrought iron bench at their yard sale.

When adding another puzzle piece--while visiting an antique store my sister, Diane, purchased a picture of a beautiful lady donning a large hat. She was dressed in typical 1900's attire and looked as if she could have walked on the Titanic.

My sister named her Rose not knowing that this was also my spiritual name and also the name of the leading lady in a Titanic movie. Also, pictures of ladies who lived during the early 1900's adorned the wall above my bed at my parents' home.

Before I married in September 1973, I resided for one year with my good friend, Suzanne, at her home on Hull Street in Detroit, Michigan. She had just lost her mother to brain cancer. Stricken with grief and loneliness, a roommate was just what she needed for love and support.

Her street 'Hull' corresponds to the 'starboard hull' where the iceberg struck the Titanic. Could Suzanne have joined Gregory and me on that ill-fated ship? They are first cousins and my close friends. There were nearly 1,500 souls that perished that night.

Several years ago, I took a hypnosis class. Hypnotherapy had always amazed me, but it wasn't until the fourth session that I saw results. While drifting into a dream-like trance, my subconscious began to take over, and I found myself inside what seemed to be in a large ship. While lying in a fancy canopy bed, a small dog appeared on the floor at the foot of the bed. Though small, he had a loud bark. Although short-lived, it was a memorable event. Was this dog named Kitty? Kitty was the name of the Airedale dog that accompanied Mr. and Mrs. John Jacob Astor on the Titanic. It's interesting to note that my sister's cat was also named Kitty. One might say that 'Kitty' is a typical cat name, but that is rarely the case.

Speaking of subconscious memories, looking back in November of 1998, I dreamt I was on a ship, when the cabin began to fill with water, forcing me to climb on the bed. Was this a past life memory?

In 1996 my good friend, Thelma, and I visited a bookstore. We asked the store clerk if there were any books about spirituality. He suggested a popular book entitled "Small Miracles", where each story describes a true life situation that ends in a miraculous coincidence. The price was inexpensive so I purchased one copy for each of us. The stories were very interesting, yet difficult to believe.

As I read about the Titanic, my heart skipped a beat. This account describes a fictitious book entitled, "The Titan," written twelve years before the Titanic sank. The Titan, a ship that sank in the Atlantic Ocean, had strange parallels to the Titanic. The length of the Titan was 800 feet, the Titanic was 882.5 and both used three propellers. The Titan's speed at impact with the iceberg was 25 knots; the Titanic's 23.

Also, the book listed the total number of passengers at 2,207. Reading that number sent chills down my spine, because this number has been a part of my life for as long as I can remember. 2207 has appeared on street addresses, doctor bills, phone bills, telephone numbers, and check numbers. Even while alive, my deceased ex-husband, Michael Stemmer, had the number 2207 appear often in his life. I began to wonder if the real reason I bought this book was to allow me to travel to another dimension that would reveal this unforgettable past life.

When married, my second address was 34450 Preston Drive. Please see 450 and the word 'ton'--the Titanic weighed approximately 45, 000 tons. The other 4 could mean Boat 4 on which Madeleine had been rescued. My friend Suzanne's address was 20450 Hull Street. My grandmother's address was 4500 Island Park Drive on Woodhull Lake.

My nephew, Michael John, wife Santina, and their daughters, Melina and Diana reside on Southampton Street in Michigan. The Titanic had journeyed from Southampton, England to New York. The numbers 6462 in his address, remarkably are in the Astor's cabin number- 6264. Looking at a previous address of Michael, we see the numbers 6782. As stated earlier, John Astor's net worth was $87 million. His cemetery lot was 743-786. In both cases we see the numbers 87, and 6 is in the lot number. Also, his phone numbers have 43 and 86. Lastly, to call Michael, I first dial 1248-- the number 124 was given to identify Astor's body after it was taken from the open sea.

Recently while speaking to Michael, who is a financial advisor, he said "Someday I'll be a millionaire." Also, my sister was surprised when he looked out at Woodhull Lake in December, 2012, and said, "With it being so cold and windy, I can't imagine what it was like for the people on the Titanic going into that bitterly cold water." We wondered why he said that at the time I was writing this story because he wasn't aware of this book. Could it be that Michael was John Jacob Astor in another existence? After all, John is his middle name. Lately, while looking at a picture on my kitchen table of Michael and I walking together in New York City--where the Astors' had lived, I noticed the number 448 on a sign. 4 is April and 4+8=12-- the month and year the Titanic sank.

Observing the letters in my name "Michele Novak Stemmer", we see the name "Astor". Also, my last name is noteworthy; I can't tell you how many times I have been called Miss Steamer, instead of Miss Stemmer. This is another reminder to me of the world's largest steamship- Titanic.

Another example would be the woman named Brooke Russell Marshall. She was married to William Vincent Astor who was John Jacob Astor's son with his first wife Ava Willing. It excites me to share that my niece, Lisa Marshall Wylin and her husband James, have two daughters, Kristina and Brooke Marshall Wylin. Brooke's birthdate is June 19, the same as Madeleine's, and Brooke's name is close to William Astor's wife. Also, the birthdate of William Vincent Astor was November 15, which is the same as my granddaughter, Jennifer Lynn Stemmer's birthday.

On a side note, when I went shopping at Winn-Dixie in South Carolina, I noticed the word ASTOR on a salad dressing bottle. Also, I noticed on a sign next to the road that Greenville is the sister city of Bergamo (as in iceberg) Italy.

One more example is when I spent a month with my family in Waterford, Michigan during Christmas. Since my parents were up in age, I offered to help with the housework. One day while washing the dishes, the 'sink' began to plug up. The metal strainer's holes were large, so I thought it wise to use strainers with smaller holes to help prevent food particles from getting into the drain. I went to a kitchen and bath store hoping to find other strainers but none were available, and could only be ordered through the catalog. I left, thinking I would find a strainer elsewhere.

As I approached my car, I was unable to get inside because the car next to me was parked too close. There was a lady in that car talking on the cell phone. I waited for awhile, but she still wasn't ready to leave. My patience began to wear thin, so I went to Murray's Auto Store, to purchase a bottle of car oil for my father. When I walked down the aisle, another past life encounter came before me.

12

I noticed SOS on a box of soap pads...another reminder of the Titanic's signals for help.

Did noticing the problem with the sink somehow, in my mind, correspond with the memory of the Titanic sinking? Why did I turn to see the SOS soap pads? SOS was the signal the Titanic used to contact the Carpathia- the ship that rescued the survivors.

Never before have I had such a profound experience in my life as I did in Greenville, South Carolina where I believe I relived a portion of a past life as Madeleine Force Astor. It also seemed clear to me that the spiritual reason was to be led there to experience through various events, memories of my time on the ill-fated steamship called the Titanic. It's possible that this was my most recent past lifetime, which explains why there are so many memories available to me now. In the beginning of this true story, I explained that my son wanted to move from Michigan to the South in order to find a school that had a later start time. Well, it's true but that was only the material or physical reason. The real or spiritual reason, however, was for my sake.

The Titanic rests near Newfoundland, Canada, in an area where oxygen and saltwater are unusually high. Wood boring worms had eaten away almost all of the wood. The ship lies in 13,000 feet of water on the gently sloping, alpine-like countryside. The bow faces north and the ship sits upright on the bottom. It is very dark at this depth and is quiet and peaceful.

Fifteen years have passed since my "Titanic Connection" took place, but I still think about it often. My dream came true when Divine guidance came forth enabling me to write this story on the 100th anniversary of the sinking of the Titanic.

Sandy Hook Angels

When my daughter-in-law Laurel came over to help me on December 14, 2012 she asked, ''Did you hear about the shootings?'' ''No, I have not listened to the news yet today.'' I replied as I immediately turned on the television and listened to reports about the shootings at Sandy Hook Elementary school in Newtown, Connecticut. When I heard that twenty children between five and eight years of age and five teachers had been killed, shock and sadness overwhelmed my heart. Who would commit such a horrific act?

In the days that followed, further investigation determined that the gunman was mentally unstable and had apparently killed his mother and took his own life. It was quite surprising to learn that she owned these assault weapons used by the gunman. They had gone together to a shooting range to practice--though it wasn't clear how often they had practiced.

I then began to put together and analyze what transpired for two days before this happened which would clarify what the real or spiritual reason was behind this tragedy.

1. At 9:00 a.m. Thursday, December 13, I had the television on in my bedroom. The news report stated that three schools were closing that day but did not explain why. It didn't seem reasonable to close the schools because the weather was fine.

2. On December 14, I was typing my 9/11 story with information about a tragedy and children.

3. On December 14, a friend, Cecelia Cole, called whom I just got reacquainted with about a month before. During our conversation, she stated that she was a school teacher.

4. On December 14, another friend had called and mentioned that plans had changed because his client had died. He was going to the funeral home instead of seeing a movie. It wasn't necessary for him to call and explain- Was this a message from Spirit?

To interpret the clues above, we see the words school, tragedy, children, teacher, and died.

This incident touched the lives of many people throughout our country and the world. As with other tragedies, people reach out to lend a helping hand. Our President, Barack Obama, shed tears and was determined to find a solution for gun violence.

I believe these children and teachers did not die in vain. Statistics show that more people die from gun violence than car accidents. In light of this, our government and American people have said enough is enough. Maybe these people lost their lives so others could be saved.

We now see security being increased in schools. For example, my friend went to her granddaughter's high school and had to sign in and state her reason for visiting. I'm sure other schools in America are following similar procedures.

There is now a push for the U.S. Congress to pass a bill on gun safety legislation. Citizens started groups advocating to stop this violence. Thousands even demonstrated in Washington, D.C.

During this ordeal, the Newtown Police Department had been exceptionally busy. With the 2012 Christmas season fast approaching, a neighboring community police department decided to voluntarily take over the duties of these police officers for a couple of days.

Shipments of toys were brought in to help the grieving families. People all over the United States and other countries throughout the world were sending monetary donations for victims' families in Newtown, Connecticut.

In California they had a 'Guns for Groceries' project. Anyone could bring guns to the grocery store and receive a $100 certificate per gun to be used for groceries. There were 2.000 firearms brought in for this cause.

I was truly amazed to discover another parallel with this tragic situation. Two months ago, in October, 2012, we remember the terrifying effects and aftermath of Hurricane Sandy. Both tragedies bear the name Sandy and have the same initials S and H. I believe these two events happened close together emphasizing God's message for all humanity to help one another in time of need. We see the general public sending love through gifts, money, volunteering their time and most of all prayer. The Sandy Hook tragedy concerned small children, so the outpouring of loving support from everyone was even greater.

On a personal note, I had heard that on the day of the tragedy the children were going to make gingerbread houses which obviously did not happen. In memoriam to them, I handmade a Christmas card for my son and daughter-in-law adorned with a gingerbread house and gingerbread boy. Also, my family made a gingerbread house to display every Christmas in memory of not only the children who lost their lives, but the others who suffered emotional trauma when they lost their classmates.

Noticing the school's name, Sandy Hook, we see the words 'Sad' and 'Ok'. I believe through these words, Spirit is telling us as 'sad' as this was, it will be 'okay.' To help one feel better, we can see the good that has come from something bad. Let us be assured that those who lost their lives are now receiving tender loving care on the other side.

9/11 Revisited

Surely, all of us remember where we were on September 11, 2001-- The day when four jets were hijacked, two crashed into the World Trade Center towers in New York City, one into the Pentagon and one into the Pennsylvania countryside. At least 3,000 people were killed. Not since the assassination of President Kennedy has something hit me so hard. These events will never be forgotten.

As I awoke that morning while at my parents' home in Waterford, I sat in horror as these events unfolded on television. I remember the shock that went through my body like a bolt of lightning. It didn't seem real, and appeared as if we were watching a terrifying movie about hijacked jetliners. We were later informed that this was the work of terrorists from Afghanistan, another despicable deed of Osama bin Laden and al- Qaeda. However, in the past several years there has been a controversy about who was responsible for this terrorist attack.

Later that day, I considered if there were any clues lately that would have warned me that this terrible tragedy would take place.

1. Went to a party at Camp Dearborn in Michigan where I was a face painter. Most of the people were from Iraq. The lady giving the party was named Bina (as in 'bin' Laden).

2. At the party stated above, I had drawn several stars on children's faces. It seemed strange that so many children wanted a five-pointed star-- I've never painted so many at one party. I believe the message related to the Pentagon which is a five- sided building.

3. On September 10, I delivered toner to a nearby business. The time was 11:11 on the van clock. Seeing 11 twice, could be a 9/11 message.

4. While sitting in my van, I closed my eyes and envisioned several jets in the sky.

5. As I left Good Food Company Health Food store, there was a man with a long beard that looked like bin Laden who walked by me as he was going in the store.

6. Noticed a sticker on a shirt that had the numbers 119.

7. Had focused on the street sign Arlington. Arlington, Virginia is where the Pentagon is located.

Even though this information was important, unfortunately it was not enough for me to predict or forewarn anyone that this nightmare would be happening.

Inauguration Day

On Inauguration Day, 2013, I was anxious to see President Obama get sworn in for a second term just before 12:00 noon. My home health care aide was also due to be here about the same time. I had hoped that she would come later so I would be able to watch the early inaugural festivities. I felt relieved when Shawn called and said she would arrive about 1:00 p.m.

Upon arriving, she said the reason for being late was because she had to see a new client. Shawn was upset because the lady had already taken a bath and did not need any other help. She also felt that she drove there for nothing and hoped for compensation for her time and mileage.

In this situation, something good came from something bad. When Shawn suffered and had to be diverted temporarily, I could finish watching the inaugural festivities.

Predictions

To make a prediction, I pay attention to words, names, numbers, bottles, mail, television ads, people, objects, etc. in my life and often take it to the extreme so no stone is left unturned.

1. While living in Tallahassee, Florida, I happened to notice a street sign called 'Raymond Diehl'. Looking at the name 'Raymond' reminded me of my cousin Raymond-then I noticed 'Die' in the word Diehl. I wondered if this was a message that my cousin Raymond would die soon because I noticed this sign a few times. We did get word of his passing two years later. I spoke with his daughter and she explained that he was healthy up until two months before his demise which made my prediction credible. He had gone in the hospital for knee replacement surgery and contracted MRSA, a bad infection which didn't respond to the treatment, hence he passed away.

2. My dad was devastated while watching my bed-ridden mother as she suffered with her illness. One day while I was feeding her, he said ''I'm waiting for you sweetheart.''Another time he mentioned there would be a change. After dinner, I felt because we kept 'crossing over' the highway several times, this

had a special meaning. One time I forgot something at a restaurant, so I pulled into the driveway of their future cemetery to turn around and head back to the restaurant. I felt after seeing the above events transpire, my father would be leaving this earth soon. When he said, "I'm waiting for you sweetheart", it meant that he was going to pass away first. Saying there would be a 'change' is the spiritual word for death. The words "crossing over" also means to leave the earth plane. My turning into the driveway wasn't a coincidence; it was a message. I was correct with my prediction because this happened about three months before my father's demise, in January, 2003. My mother transitioned in April, 2003, three months later.

3. Within two months before my father passed away in 2003, I had gone to a drive through oil – change station. As I sat in my car, noticing several men quickly performing an oil change, what immediately came to my mind was there would be many people around my father in his home helping him... probably paramedics. My father at age 85, was not ill at the time, but about a week later he suffered from the flu. Initially, he didn't want to go to the hospital but his condition got worse, so we called an ambulance. It turned out that there were eight paramedics working on him at his home. I walked out of the house crying and said "I knew this was going to happen."

4. On February 27, 2010, when my scooter had stalled in my walk-in closet in Tallahassee, I said, ''I'm chilly.'' My roommate Becca, suffering from the flu, replied she was getting chills. It soon came to me that there would be an earthquake in Chile-- I was correct, an 8.8 magnitude earthquake occurred that day. Also,

I felt something would happen with countries that started with the letter 'A'. It turned out the countries Argentina, Asia, Australia, and America had felt some tremors that day.

5. On October 9, 2010, I had a strange feeling about a country beginning with the letter I--either Indonesia or India. On October 25, 2010 there was a 7.7 earthquake in Sumatra, Indonesia, plus a volcano eruption and tsunami.

6. As I sat up in bed the morning of October 1, 2011, the word gargantuan (which means huge) came into my mind. Later that day I looked into a storage bin in my family room and noticed on a newspaper that read 5 days and next to it word 'danger'. My message indicated that in 5 days something significant would happen. On October 6, something did happen. There was a suspicious package discovered at the Capitol Building in Washington, DC.--they even closed down Pennsylvania Avenue. They were unable to x-ray the package because it was very dense. It was determined the object looked like a pipe with end caps and wires sticking out of it –a possible grenade. It was sent to Quantico, Virginia to be checked by a bomb squad. It was found to be a piece of equipment used to inspect sewer pipes. There also was a 6.2 magnitude earthquake in Argentina. It should be noted that the word gargantuan could relate to another event in the near future not necessarily what occurred on October 6, 2011.

7. The morning of October 9, 2011, as I arose the words 'epic proportions' came to my mind. The next day I noticed my supplement was called 'Epic'. Five days

later an advertisement on television had mentioned 'epic proportion.' I felt that something big would be happening very soon because these words came to me three times in a row. On October 16, there was an underwater volcano eruption in El Hierro, Canary Islands. On October 20, there were three small earthquakes in California. Texas also had an earthquake that day. On October 22, there was an earthquake in Turkey.

8. At the end of September, 2012, I saw the words 'The Big One' on a washcloth tag in my linen closet. Every time I opened the door, the words 'The Big One' stared at me for three weeks. As with other predictions, when I am shown the word 'Big' it means a tragedy will soon happen. This was confirmed because the washcloth just happened to be in the same place for a month. When I heard the news of Hurricane Sandy on October 25, this message made sense. Also, just before this happened, I thought about a girl named Sandy who was my childhood neighbor. It may sound silly to get messages from the tags on washcloths, but the day before the tsunami in Japan on March 11, 2011, I noticed the words 'The Big One' on my washcloth tag.

9. In February, 2013, the word 'epic' had been shown to me several times in various ways. For example, epic video, epic holiday sale, epic fun adventure, epic taste from a cereal company, epic vacation in Florida and epic television series. The definition of epic is surpassing the ordinary in size or scale. The number 27 was also shown to me a few times. 27th Precinct appeared on an old "Law and Order" television show. Noticed 27 many times on a list of numbers used

for my health. There were 27 pads in a new package in my linen closet. It was mentioned on television there would be 27 spiritual shows. These clues prompted me to believe we can expect a major event-possibly an earth calamity on March 27, 2013.

On the news that evening it was reported that there was a massive landslide in the state of Washington. Also, they announced that North Korea was threatening to attack the United States and also cut off communication with South Korea. Another report stated that there is an 'epic' cultural war going on regarding same sex marriages. These three events prompted me to believe my prediction with accurate especially because the word 'epic' was included.

10. On April 10, 2013, while watching television, the furniture commercial said "The Big One" referring to a huge sale. Later that day, I heard the word 'Epic'. The same day a package came in the mail with the numbers 97, 98, and 99 that really resonated with me. Also, I saw the letter 'T' on a dish with blueberries-- this could stand for terrorist attack or Texas. I noticed a long and narrow covered object in my neighbor's yard which my psychic eye interpreted as a missile to detonate a bomb. A friend from a town near Iraq came over to help me on the exact same day and time of the Boston bombings.

Therefore, I believed the suspects were from another country and there was also some connection with Iraq. The media announced that the suspects were against the war in Afghanistan and Iraq.

Seeing all these messages revealed to me that big events would take place on April 16 (adding 9+7) through

26

possibly April 17 (adding 9+8) or April 18 (9+9). On April 15, a bomb exploded at the finish line during the Boston Marathon. On April 16 there was a big 7.8 magnitude earthquake in Iran. On April 17, there were suspicious letters containing ricin poison sent to a senator and our U.S President. Also that day, the Senate rejected legislation on background checks for assault weapons. The same evening there was a huge explosion at a fertilizer plant in Texas. I did see fire on an advertisement sent in the mail and intuitively felt there would be an explosion. I believed much tension from these tragedies would be felt across the country for at least six days, possibly more. Most of my predictions were accurate.

Chapter II

Spiritual Encounters

Saint Phanourious

Just before my divorce was final in 1994, I was diagnosed with breast cancer. I spent about one year agonizing while dealing with this health condition. It was very comforting to get acquainted with St. Phanourious Greek Orthodox church during this time.

I took the conventional treatments and was fortunate to give myself injections in my legs to keep my immune system in check. I also had used alternative protocols. Through my research, I found out that with stage 2 breast cancer, there is a good chance for recovery. I am proud to say that I have been a cancer survivor for nineteen years and counting.

I started going to Saint Phanourious because I felt the need to pray and also give thanks to God that I was still alive. Recently, they had just moved this church close to my house-- a mile away. This Saint was known to have healed many people. I am confident that my healing came from both Saint Phanourious and my alternative treatments.

Also, when someone had lost something, they would ask him for help and would soon recover the lost item. Little is known about him except that he died a martyr after having been horribly tortured.

Instead of statues, the Greek Orthodox religion has a variety of icons in their churches. A band of roving Arabs uncovered ruins of an ancient Greek Orthodox church and found icons in near ruin except for Saint Phanourious which appeared looking new and fresh as if just painted. It was concluded that this Saint was a man of divine grace. He became the patron saint of things lost because he was lost for centuries in the ruins of a church.

For three years, I continued to visit the church almost on a daily basis. I would go alone or sometimes bring a family member or friend. It's difficult to describe the wondrous and peaceful feeling that encompasses your soul when you walk into this holy church. Incidentally, when living in the Bible Belt, in South Carolina, I attended twelve different churches. I am pleased to say that compared to these places of worship, Saint Phanourious had a beautiful mystique like no other.

My good friend Thelma also loved going to church with me. When I first met Thelma through a mutual friend I had dated, we soon began talking about Saint Phanourious. She had gone to church in Roseville, Michigan before it was relocated near me. I believe our friendship blossomed because we were both very spiritual and had many things in common, especially this church. I often visited her at home and had spent the night a couple of times. Occasionally, we had gone out to dinner together.

After a couple of years, unfortunately the church had to be moved again. The priest explained to me they could not afford the rent for that building. We were astounded that they moved four blocks from Thelma's home. It was also near my home-- five miles away. We would often go during the day and sit and pray in an empty church because there would not be a service until evening.

It was such a miracle that a halo appeared around Saint Phanourious. This 'fog- like' halo was first discovered in 1991, when a cleaning lady began to clean the icon and was unable to wipe off what looked like a mist around his head.

Recently, my health practitioner asked me if I was of Mediterranean descent because my test result was characteristic of that area. I explained that I was not from that region. Later that day, I began to think that I could have lived in Greece in a past life because I felt such a strong connection with this Greek Orthodox church. During my childhood, I was also asked if I was of Greek descent.

Attending St. Phanourious church was a very reward- ing experience. Not only was he a Saint; to me he appeared as a friend.

I believe this church moved from another location at the perfect time to give me hope during a health crisis. Also, it provided an opportunity to get to know Thelma. Lately, I have been reminded of her because I reflect upon the words she used to say: 'Be wise like a serpent and harmless as a dove', and 'Cast out your troubles into the sea of forgetfulness'.

The Steamed Mirror

One day as I stepped out of the shower, I looked up and noticed the word ''GOD'' on my steamed bathroom mirror. At first I thought that I could be imagining this, so I decided to leave the mirror alone until my friends could see it.

A couple of days later my friends Suzanne and Liz came over. I turned the bathtub water on and the steam covered the mirror as it had two days before. We looked and noticed the word "GOD". They agreed that it looked like someone had printed his Holy Name.

Was this a simple way to show me that God was always with me? God communicates with us in many different ways.

Psalm 23

The Lord is My Shepherd (Psalm 23) came into my life many times during the late 1990's. Psalm 23 written below and some of my interesting experiences with this Biblical passage are recounted here.

Psalm 23: The Lord is My Shepherd, I shall not want. He maketh me to lie down in green pastures: he leadeth me beside the still waters. He restoreth my soul: He leadeth me in the paths of righteousness for his name's sake. Yea, though I walk through the valley of the shadow of death, I will fear no evil; for thou art with me; thy rod and thy staff they comfort me. Thou preparest a table before me in the presence of mine enemies; thou anointest my head with oil; my cup runneth over. Surely goodness and mercy shall follow me all the days of my life: and I will dwell in the house of the Lord forever.

A Radio Broadcast:

One Sunday evening I was at my parents' home in Waterford, Michigan preparing to spend the night. My niece, Lisa, had her baby shower that day and I didn't want to make the trip home. My son Marc called about 8:30 p.m. wondering why I had not returned home. He misunderstood me when I explained that I would be staying overnight. Hearing his anxiety, I reluctantly drove home.

While driving, I listened to a classical radio station where a speaker from a Unity church gave an inspiring talk.

She spoke of God always being there for you and to ask for his guidance whenever necessary; that we are all spiritual beings on a mission. She also mentioned that a well known minister had said, "When you want something, don't give up on it." The most important message was when she referred to Psalm 23, "The Lord is My Shepherd." Jesus has set an example and we too can be like him. Immediately it occurred to me why I had driven home that night. The reason being was to hear that special message and perhaps answer my question--"Am I part of Jesus' flock?"

A Spiritual Book:

While grocery shopping at a store in Sterling Heights, Michigan, I noticed a spiritual book on a bookrack. I removed the book and just happened to open to the page that had Psalm 23.

Grandmother Julia:

My grandmother, Julia Dingel, had passed away on June 18, 1997. On the morning of her demise, I happened to turn on the radio to a religious station where I heard the commentator begin reciting Psalm 23. While listening to his captivating voice which was enhanced by the mystique of the background music, I felt guided to record his message-- never to be erased from the tape or from my memory. It was very rewarding and a comfort to hear this at the time I mourned for my precious grandmother.

The movie "Titanic:

The movie "Titanic" also had a special meaning to me. Not only did it show some of the people recite Psalm 23 while waiting to perish on this ill-fated steamer, but it also brought back memories of a possible past life as Madeleine Force Astor.

The Meditation Room:
   My friend Marie was upset because her husband Edwin was ill and taken to the hospital. She doesn't drive, so she asked me to take her to the hospital to see him. After a nice visit, we went through the main lobby to leave the hospital. Before we reached the door, I noticed a meditation room. Though small, it was a beautiful room, with an altar donned with flowers and a Bible. I began to read Psalm 23 because the Bible was opened to the Psalm section.

Shepherd's Gate:
   While living in Greenville, South Carolina also known as the "Bible Belt"...I was told this city had more churches per capita than anywhere in the country. One day while taking a ride around the city, I noticed a homeless shelter called Shepherd 's Gate. Curious about this place because of its interesting name, I walked in and was astonished when I viewed a picture on the wall that said Psalm 23, "The Lord is My Shepherd".

Fraser Library:
   One day I went shopping at a nearby grocery store located in Fraser, Michigan. On the way home I drove through a cemetery. As I turned left from the main road, I noticed a gravesite that had a book standing with pink flowers. On the book it read ''The Lord is my Shepherd, I shall not want... He leadeth me to still waters."

A Gift:

My friend Suzanne had sent me a birthday card with a refrigerator magnet that said Psalm 23 ''The Lord is My Shepherd''. She was unaware of my other messages received about this Psalm.

I believe Psalm 23 had been shown to me so many times to signify that we are the sheep and Jesus is our Shepherd and we can count on him to always be there to watch over us.

Gabriel, Michael, and Daniel

As discussed in the Titanic story, I had gone shopping at Murray's Auto Store and saw SOS soap pads-- a reminder of the signal to contact the Carpathia ship to rescue survivors.

While walking down the aisle, I noticed a very familiar and beautiful word Gabriel. My first thought was "Did this mean Archangel Gabriel?" Looking at the physical side, Gabriel was the name of a certain tool company. Of course, the real or spiritual side was the name of an Archangel. Gabriel has come into my life many times through the years. I see his name often-- even the cosmetics I use come from a company called Gabriel.

As I continued down the next aisle, to my surprise, I saw my nephew Michael (as in Michael the Archangel) and his friend Daniel (as in Daniel the Prophet). I thought if I keep looking, perhaps a bible would soon appear. Of course, I am only joking.

Daniel explained that he was living in Greenville, South Carolina and lived off of White Horse Road. The road was very familiar to me because I had worked for a company located on White Horse Road. In the Bible: Revelation, Chapter 19: verse 11 states--Then I saw heaven open and there was a white horse. It's rider is called Faithful and True; it is with justice that he judges and fights his battles. The words White Horse Road is physical and the above Revelation message is spiritual.

Daniel explained that he had worked for the same company where I had been given a temporary assignment as a switchboard operator. Also, we discovered that we both had registered with the same temporary agency, and had even spoken to the same agent.

That evening Michael gave me Daniel's phone number. Months later his phone number which had 767 offered a clue to the Egyptian Airplane crash.

During my stay in Greenville, many events of my life had exceptional parallels with the Book of Daniel. This made me wonder if I could have been Daniel at another time or a prophet that walked with him. The day before I met Daniel at Murray's, I had mentioned to my parents that I was starting to feel like a prophet because sometimes I can see the future-- Seeing Daniel at the store seemed to confirm this. Also, I had just read my father's book stating many facts about Daniel who was born 600 years before Christ.

Bringing these Archangels together with Daniel corresponds to the Book of Daniel in the Bible. Gabriel explains Daniel 's vision which refers to the time of the end-- Daniel Chapter 7 verses 20-23. Gabriel had come to Daniel to help him understand a prophecy. Michael the Archangel said he was considered Israel's guardian angel. He was responsible for helping and defending Daniel. Michael came to Daniel to reveal what is written in the Book of Truth.

Seeing each other at Christmas was a special time to connect. Did the fact that we met at this location mean that we were together in another existence? Perhaps we worked together in another lifetime because my friend Daniel and I had similar work experiences.

Angel at the Beach

It was a warm October day in Tallahassee, Florida, so my son Marc, daughter-in-law Laurel, and I went to a beach in the Gulf of Mexico to go swimming. I had to be taken to the ocean in a wheelchair. They wheeled me right into the water so the large waves hit my legs and arms. It was very refreshing and magical to feel this saltwater surround my body. So much so, that I also gathered some water in a bottle to take home to pamper my body later.

About an hour later we headed back to the van to go home. Our van was equipped with an electrically powered chair. When we pushed a button, it came out so I could sit down easily; then we pushed another button for the chair to go back in the van. As Marc and Laurel began to load me into the van, I sat down as usual and pressed the button to go back into the van, but it would not move.

A young man with beautiful blue eyes and bare-chest came up from the beach and started talking to us. He offered his assistance, seeing that we were having trouble with my chair. He lifted me off the chair onto the wheelchair, then got down on the ground, and proceeded to help. He and Marc worked together to manually push the seat into the van. He gave it all he could, but the chair moved only slightly. He called his father for assistance and a short time later his father arrived to lend a hand.

41

In the meantime, this blond blue-eyed angel wheeled me to the other side of the van to get me out of the sun. He then went back to the chair; and together, they kept trying to get the chair inside the van. They could only move it a little more, but were able to take a strap and attach the chair to the door. He lifted me into the back seat of the van. We asked him for his address to send him some money for helping, but he refused saying he just wanted to do a good deed.

We then left for home. Unfortunately, it was very windy because the door was partly open, so I covered my head and body with a blanket. Despite being cold and very uncomfortable, we made it home safely.

Was this young man there to help us at the time we needed him? There were very few people on the beach that day. He seemed especially caring during this ordeal. I really appreciated when he lifted me off the chair on to the wheelchair and later into the van. If he wasn't there to put me in the van, my son and daughter-in-law would have had a difficult time doing so because of their back troubles. I believe he was an angel coming to our aid. I have heard that angels often times have blue eyes.

The Shoelace

In the summer of 1998, my first visit back to Michigan after moving to South Carolina, we had unusually warm weather. My parents lived on Woodhull Lake in Waterford where I often liked to swim. One day while putting on my bathing suit to go swimming, I noticed that my bathing suit strap was missing. I thought to myself, ''It would be nice if I could find a long shoelace to tie around my neck as a strap.'' I looked around the house, but none were available. I went swimming anyway hoping to find a lace later. I was only in the water a few minutes when I looked down to find a long black shoelace floating right next to me. At once I started to tie it around my neck. It was perfect and just the right length.

Finding the shoelace was surely a miracle. The shoelace could have floated anywhere on the lake. Why did it float right next to me at the exact time I needed it? Did spirit already know I would be asking for it, so it was ready for me to pick up out of the water?

Three Nuns and a Lady

My friend Marie and I went shopping at the mall. As lunch time rolled around, we decided to have a bite to eat at a restaurant in the mall. A few minutes after we ordered, two Catholic nuns walked in, sitting down in the booth directly behind me. As we passed by them to leave, my eye immediately noticed the cross around the neck of one of the nuns.

Afterward, we went to get Marie's medical prescription. I dropped her off and went to find a parking space, when to my surprise, a third nun appeared walking toward me.

Next, we headed to a local restaurant so Marie could satisfy her sweet tooth on one of their delicious desserts. A middle-aged lady kept dozing off in the booth in front of us. We asked the waitress about her, and she told us that the lady was homeless and frequented the restaurant often. The waitress offered to buy dinner for the lady, but she refused-saying she wasn't hungry.

As we continued to talk to the homeless lady, we asked where she was going, and she replied, ''I have nowhere to go to spend the night.''

We told her about a Catholic church down the street that would gladly give her shelter, and she even accepted our offer to drive her to the church. The waitress, realizing that the lady must have been starving by then, ordered her a dinner. "I'll pay for your dinner, and while you're eating, I'll call someone from the church to pick you up," she said. The waitress assured us that since the Saturday night Mass was underway, there would be someone available to come and get her. We agreed to this arrangement because my son was waiting for me-- everything seemed to fall into place.

Seeing three nuns within an hour seemed surreal-- especially because it was away from a church atmosphere. Were these holy ladies supposed to cross my path so spirit could confirm that we four were special children of the Universe? Were we meant to be there for the homeless lady? We would have gladly driven her to the church, if necessary. All three of these instances, each relating to a church or perhaps a divine calling, occurred on the same day.

Lutheran Hour Ministries

I asked for answers to help me cope with difficulties with my teenage son. The radio station at work advertised the "Lutheran Hour Ministries". When I called, they said they would send me a free copy of a book and cassette tape dealing with teens and how to deal with such things as peer pressure, drugs, alcohol abuse, and discipline. I found this material very informative and helpful.

Remember to follow a well known Bible verse in Matthew 7:7. Ask and you shall receive. seek, and you will find; knock, and the door will be opened to you.

Angels Appear

Many times angels take on human form to assist us when we call to them. They often suddenly appear out of nowhere, do a good deed or remove us from danger, then vanish very quickly. Many people have shared stories confirming this phenomenon.

One winter day I had gone to a local health food store. On the way back to my condo I stopped at my mailbox. As I reached in to get my mail, an important letter dropped on the ground. Because I parked so close to these mailboxes, it was difficult to get out of the car. Also, I was not walking well, so pulling up and walking back to retrieve the mail would have been difficult. I started to pray for someone to come and pick up the letter. All of a sudden, a lady came up to my car and asked, ''Could I get your mail?'' I remarked, ''Yes, you're an angel.'' She was there right when I needed her.

On another occasion, I rode my scooter to the mailbox to gather my mail. Everything went well until I reached my condo. I entered the garage, and while getting off the scooter, my arm touched the lever, making the scooter move so fast that it fell on top of me. Luckily, a neighbor walking her dog came by at the exact time this happened. When she saw my predicament, she came over quickly and proceeded to remove the scooter off of me. I was very grateful that she was there because I wasn't strong enough to lift the scooter myself. Unfortunately, this ordeal gave me a backache.

The above story goes along with my theory of fate. I believe what happened was already known ahead of time. These people who seemed like angels were available to help me at the exact time I needed them... Thanks to divine intervention.

Led To The Cross

One summer day in August of 2002 my friend Marie and I went to a Sunflower Festival at the Ukrainian Cultural Center in Warren, Michigan. We sat in a tent listening to live music, watched people twirl their partners on the dance floor and enjoyed the flavorful ethnic food. Our only issue was that it was very hot, noisy and cigarette smoke was in the air. The lady seated near us suggested that we move to the end of the table for less noise and to get some fresh air. Thus, we moved closer to the tent entrance, but still felt somewhat uncomfortable.

After less than an hour, we walked outside to explore more of the festival. There wasn't much more to see, so we decided to leave. For some reason, we started walking toward the farthest side of the festival grounds. All at once, we saw Jesus on the cross. Marie said she was going to buy elephant ears and would meet me back here in a few minutes. As she left, I knelt down by the cross and began praying. I then laid down on the grass, to spend time resting at the cross with Jesus. When Marie returned, we decided to leave the festival.

Did leaving the tent sooner than expected happen for a reason? It seemed like being uncomfortable in the tent was spirit's way to beckon us to leave early and find the cross. The fact that we walked near the edge instead of the middle of the grounds which was closer to the parking lot, seemed to confirm this. I believe the physical reason was to go the festival but the real or spiritual reason was to visit Jesus.

Twilight Zone Effect

My son Marc and I moved to South Carolina in February 1998. In January, previous to our move, we visited Georgia and South Carolina to decide which state would be appropriate for our lifestyle and enable Marc to attend a high school with a later start time. This trip turned out to be a profound spiritual journey.

As we waited in the airport terminal, my eyes fell upon a young lady with a small baby who had a strong resemblance to my daughter-in-law Theresa. After boarding Flight 493, she and her family sat down behind us. I then spotted another woman who looked like my aunt Elaine. Then to my amazement, I saw a woman that resembled my son's teacher. I had to do a double take thinking the man sitting next to me was Tim--a former classmate and boyfriend. He had black hair, brown eyes, and glasses which also fit Tim's description. Also, another person came into view--a lady I thought was my co-worker Becky, except she had longer hair. Perhaps these familiar faces provided comfort because I was not fond of flying.

We rented a car when we landed in Atlanta, Georgia. As I drove down the street, I noticed a license plate that read 'Julia'--my departed grandmother's name. As we drove through Gainesville, Georgia, we found it to be too industrial combined with an unimpressive country atmosphere making it an undesirable place to live.

We spent the night at a spacious hotel in Gainesville and were able to use their telephone to make other hotel reservations. As I opened the phone book, I soon noticed these names--Timothy, Kathleen, Robert and Raymond. All four names referred to people that were recently in my life.

We also spent another night at a motel in Gainesville. The motel attendant called our room and announced, "This is Lee, I hope you find your room satisfactory." It wasn't a surprise that his name was 'Lee' because that name often shows up in my life referring to people, street names, my former Florida county, etc.

The next day we headed toward Greenville, South Carolina. We were supposed to stay in Hendersonville, North Carolina, which is near Greenville. However, when driving through Gainesville, we got lost and turned into a driveway seeing the sign 'Sara Lee' and also the building that had the same name. I believed we were not lost because seeing the name 'Lee' made me feel confident we were in the right place at the right time.

After leaving the driveway in South Carolina, we found a motel nearby where we decided to spend the night. While checking in, I spoke to a man at the counter and related that I was from Detroit, Michigan. He said he went to Pershing High school and lived on Caldwell street near 6 Mile Road in Detroit. I was stunned to hear this because I also went to Pershing High school and lived on Caldwell street near Outer Drive and Mound Road about two miles from him. He then stated another lady at the motel was from Port Huron, Michigan.

The following morning we woke up to a lovely brilliant sun in contrast with the dark gloomy skies over Georgia. We began our day traveling to Taylors and Greer--cities located near Greenville, to check out the apartments and high schools. We wanted to find Eastside High School located in Taylors, so we turned from Wade Hampton Boulevard to 'Lee' Road and came upon the high school. We then visited The Chimneys Apartment, also in Taylors, which seemed very nice--we liked the fact that every apartment had a fireplace.

Soon we were on our way to Riverside High School located in Greer. It was such a treat traveling down the road under what felt like a tunnel of trees. The view was magnificent even though you couldn't see the sky, because the trees that hung across the road on each side had blocked it. When we reached Riverside, the area had a southern country flare. Horses and cows were grazing in the field across the road and a small white church completed this picturesque scene. We went inside the school knowing it was one of the top schools in the state with a start time of 9:00 a.m. This, plus the school having a welcoming atmosphere, convinced Marc that this was the high school for him.

On our last day, we stopped at Hampton Forest Apartments...the address was 2207 Wade Hampton Boulevard. The number 2207 has shown up in my life for years. Upon entering, I was greeted by a female receptionist whose last name was 'Lee.' After getting information, I went back to my car and noticed a woman who happened to be parked next to us. Her car was running just as I got into my car... it almost seemed like she was waiting for me. We asked her for directions to the expressway so we could return to Atlanta. She replied, ''I'm going that way anyway, so follow me.'' We then followed her to the expressway.

While on the expressway, we noticed a car following us for the majority of the trip from Greenville to Smyrna, Georgia. When it finally passed us, we followed that car the rest of the way to the airport. As we drove, I called a moving service and read on the phone ID, the word ''Kellee.'' Yet another 'Lee' which, I believe, indicated we were still on the right track.

This trip awakened me to the fact that we can be reminded of people in our lives wherever we go. For example, this trip involved nine names of people I am presently acquainted with and my deceased grandmother Julia. It was easy to decipher that the dark clouds in Georgia were an omen not to move there and the bright sun in South Carolina indicated this was the best place to live. The word 'Lee' was constantly around me and seemed to validate I was on the right path. Was it fate that we went to this certain motel to meet the employee who was from Detroit? Was the lady an angel waiting to help us find the expressway? Also, the other car appeared available for us to follow the rest of the way. Even though at times it felt like the 'Twilight Zone', I knew that the Universe was with us on this trip from start to finish.

Heaven Sent

One evening my son and I had planned to see a school play. Due to a disagreement between us, I left in a hurry without him. In the lobby I noticed a sign, ''SOLD OUT'' and a man nearby needing a ticket. He bought my son's ticket saying, "This was Heaven Sent". I rushed into the auditorium seating myself just as the curtain rose. I believe that the disagreement created this timely flow from a 'heavenly force' meant to help another. Another meaning would be something good came from something bad.

My awareness of the above situation and many others reveals to me, as a seeker, that the Universe is calling, knocking on my door. At times I feel chosen-- one of Jesus' flock. From these awakenings I'm being transformed, nurtured, and loved. I feel on an eternal mission that is bringing me great joy and meaning as one of God's special children.

Visiting Other Dimensions

In the spring of 2006, I invited my family to take part in a seance at my condominium. This was the second time I had conducted a seance. The first time was with my neighbor in South Carolina in 1998. She wanted to contact her deceased father. After saying a prayer, we asked him to give a sign that he was around. Suddenly, we heard a loud crash coming from her closet. We felt that this could have been a way her father was answering our request. The second exciting séance experience took place at my Michigan condo.

While sitting at the table, we held hands, said a prayer, and asked any departed friends or relatives to join us. All at once a loud sound came from the balcony. It sounded like a large bird, possibly a dove, flapping its wings. My cousin Cindy said ''I bet that was George making his presence known''. George, who was Cindy's husband, had recently made his transition. My cousin Eileen felt the presence of her father Bruno. I felt my uncle Alex was with us because the name Al came to mind. He had a soft spot in his heart for me, and I truly miss him. He left the earth when I was only 16 years old.

It really startled everyone when a large ball of light shot across the stairway wall and went into the kitchen and then disappeared. Then suddenly, we watched in amazement as my decorative white mini lights that surrounded the kitchen archway went off, and back on again. My cousin Andrea mentioned that she felt tapping on her chair. Also, we heard a tapping sound in the great room. Last but not least, we noticed the flame on our candle began flickering faster than normal.

It was so thrilling to see how we can visit other dimensions. Even though our departed loved ones can't actually speak to us, they use other methods to show they are around.

Chapter III

Airplane Crashes

Egyptian Air 990 Jet Crash

As I left work on October 27, 1999, I looked up in the sky and saw a jet fly right above my head. Later that day I noticed two more jets fly over my head. My sixth sense came upon the most exciting prediction I have ever had--that there would soon be an airplane crash. I was so excited that I called the airport to warn of a plane crash. This was a little premature because I was unaware of the airline until I began gathering information after it happened. Many numbers and situations in the past year had given me clues that I applied to Egyptian Air Flight 990 a Boeing 767-300ER departing from New York to Cairo, Egypt on October 31, 1999, the day of the crash.

1. My address while living in Taylors, South Carolina was 4990 Old Spartanburg Road. The flight number was 990.

2. I observed 49 and 30 on a license plate, then noticed my car clock read 3:30, while driving home from work on October 27, 1999. If we take the 9 from 49, add 3+3+3 = 9, and attach the 0, we get 990, the flight number. Furthermore, the date of the crash is 10-31-1999. The numbers 990 are seen as clear as day.

3. The phone numbers of two friends from Michigan had the number 767 which was the type of jet that crashed.

4. Marc bought the supplement St. John's Wort with the dosage of 300mg. I stared at the bottle on the table noticing 300-- one of the numbers that pertained to the Egyptian jet.

5. There were other reminders of Egypt, such as a paper pyramid at the health food store, an Egyptian poster at the library, a gas station owner named Sphinx. Lastly, the Prince of Egypt movie was playing in Greenville, South Carolina. (Why was that movie playing there at that time?...the timing was perfect.)

6. Did one of the pilots decide to take his life? The authorities had questioned that because the plane's auto-pilot was switched off. Also, when I called the apartment manager in South Carolina regarding back rent, I received crushing news that the maintenance man had taken his life. The above incident could have related to the crash, because it occurred at the same time the other clues came to me. After a thorough investigation, the cause of the crash was still not known.

Since every physical event that takes place has spiritual meaning to me, it will never be ignored. These conversations with Spirit deliver messages that make many ordinary day occurrences something noteworthy. It never ceases to amaze me how numbers help to unravel these mysteries.

Air France Concorde Flight 4590

A message came to me two days before an Air France Concorde Flight 4590 crashed into a hotel in Gonesse, France on July 25, 2000. As I walked outside and noticed a jet flying directly over my head, I felt that there would soon be an airplane crash. Messages often come to me both before and after a crash occurs.

They believe the cause of the crash was when a Continental DC-10, departing five minutes before the Concorde, lost a metal strip that fell onto the runway. This strip punctured a tire on the Concorde and bits of the tire got into the fuel tanks causing a fire that took hold of the port wing during the takeoff roll in Paris.

A couple of days after the crash, I parked my car behind my friend Ed Yurich's Concorde. While in my car, I looked up and saw the number 45 on his neighbor's trailer address, and then looked down on a piece of mail to see the number 90. There it was... the numbers together were 4590--the flight number of the Concorde jet. Also the word Concorde was clearly seen on Ed's car. When taking a different route back home from the lake, I noticed the word Concorde on an unfamiliar building.

It seems as though Spirit wants to keep me informed as before about these disasters. Unfortunately, the information is given to me too late, so I am unable to provide a warning which might have prevented them from happening.

The Concorde Jet And The Titanic

There are profound yet eerie similarities between the Air France Concorde jet that crashed on July 25, 2000, and the Titanic.

The media explained that the passengers, who were mostly Germans, were on their way to New York city to board a cruise ship called the MS Deutschland for a 16-day cruise to Manta, Equador.

The investigation revealed that a metal strip from the previous takeoff of a Continental DC-10 fell onto the runway in Paris and punctured a tire on the Concorde. Bits of tire got into the fuel tanks, started a fire and caused damage to the port wing. The accident was considered a 'hull' loss and the aircraft involved was one of the only two Concorde aircrafts to be scrapped.

Due to asymmetric thrust, the 'starboard' wing lifted, banking the aircraft to 100 degrees. The aircraft was overloaded by about a 'ton' above the maximum safe take-off weight. It was flying 2,200 kilometers per hour-- the Titanic had 2,207 passengers.

I noticed that in both cases a ship was involved. The word 'port' pertains to the location where a ship has docked. In the Concorde crash, the fire damaged the port wing. John Jacob Astor, a passenger on the Titanic, went to St. Paul's school in Concord, New Hampshire. He and his wife boarded the Titanic from Cherbourg, France and were enroute back to New York City. The Concorde jet also left France and was headed back to New York City. The Titanic's full name is RMS (Royal Mail Steamer). The Concorde passengers were going to board the MS Deutschland-- MS stands for motor ship. Both ships have letters MS in their name.

Each accident involved the starboard and hull. Digits of the date of the crash, 7-25 add up to 14. The Titanic was hit by the iceberg on its starboard hull on April 14. Also, the Concorde takeoff began at 15:44, military time. The 15th of April (15/4) was the date the Titanic sunk.

My assessment seems credible because of all similarities between these two tragedies. Considering that there are many plane crashes, I wondered why I had a connection with the Air France crashes and also the Egyptian plane crash. Psychically, I sensed that I lived in France and Egypt in another lifetime and a few souls from the Titanic may have reincarnated and been aboard the Concorde jet as well.

Air France Flight 447

Since the spiritual world has no concept of time, some messages come to me close to the incident but rarely on the day of the crash. As soon as I heard about the Air France crash, I immediately started to put the information together. This Airbus A330-- Air France Flight 447 left Rio de Janeiro, Brazil en route to Paris, France on June 1, 2009, the same day it crashed. The crash was caused by speed sensors (pitot tubes) that failed after being clogged with ice sending inaccurate data to the cockpit.

As a rule, when I make a prediction, a thought or word will come to me to pay attention to. It's like a bell ringing in my mind so I know this information will have meaning about a certain event, usually tragic, will occur. Instead of calling this a prediction, this could be considered a mystery and I am the detective. These clues from Spirit describe how I solved this mystery:

1. On May 27, my son Michael and his family visited us in Florida. Feeling a little stressed, I kidded and said, "I want to move to another country, probably France."

2. On June 5, the word 'crash' came into my mind.

3. On June 6, I saw the word 'Brazil' on the tag of my bath towel.

4. On June 7, noticed while sitting at my table, the numbers 447 on a telephone number.

5. Just happened to read in the Bible, Ezekiel Chapter 41 verse 6-- These rooms were in three stories with thirty rooms on each floor. This corresponds to Airbus numbers A330.

Spirit dropped many clues which gave me a message to solve the mystery. As stated above, even though these clues came soon after the fact, the spiritual world is not limited to linear time as we are... It knows 'no time'.

Payne Stewart Learjet 35

On October 25, 1999, golfer Payne Stewart who had just won the U.S Open, had lost his life along with four other people when his Learjet 35 crashed. They left Orlando, Florida enroute to Dallas, Texas when the aircraft suddenly went on auto-pilot and crashed in a cow pasture in South Dakota. The cause of the crash could have been when the jet lost cabin pressure.

On October 24 the day before the crash, I babysat for my greatniece, Brooke. That evening I came back to my parents' home to spend the night. While watching television with my father, my eyes suddenly looked up at the grandfather clock that read 9:20. The next moment I observed the electric clock on top of the television which also had the time of 9:20--the correct time. It seemed rather peculiar that I noticed they both had the same time even though the grandfather clock was not working. I began to wonder if this was a message.

The next day, October 25, I went to register for a temporary agency. When I arrived, my first stop was the restroom. A lady started talking to me, and stated that she had heard there was a jet flying on auto-pilot and the passenger and crew were presumed dead. Later when listening to the news report in my car, they stated that the aircraft left at 9:20 a.m. and crashed at 12:25 p.m.

The following messages had come to me within a day of this crash:

1. I kept saying that I was "leery of doctors", (as in Learjet).

2. While driving the car, I had a feeling that a plane was going to crash.

3. When working as a receptionist, a man named Payne called the office.

4. I kept watching the clock as I drove down the expressway. I happened to be traveling between 12:10 and 12:50 p.m. This was near the time the plane crashed being 12:25 p.m.

5. As stated above, noticing the two clocks read 9:20 made me realize that this was the time the aircraft had departed.

For some reason, I seem to be connected to airplanes. I have lived close to airports throughout my life. When living close to a small airport in Sterling Heights, the planes would fly directly over my house.

Confrontation In The Sky

On a clear crisp evening, I wandered out of my parents' house in Waterford, Michigan to get a breath of fresh air. At the time, this had become a part of my normal pattern of behavior.

As I looked up into a beautiful starlit sky, three jets appeared. It seemed as though two were on the same course, and one veered off to the right. I came back into the house and told my father that it seemed as though there was going to be a confrontation between three countries. Intuitively, I felt that China, Taiwan, and the United States would be involved in some type of confrontation in the sky which would occur April 1, 2001.

Six months later, two Chinese jets surrounded an American jet in international airspace. One of the Chinese jets veered off and crashed after clipping the American jet's wing, killing the Chinese pilot. The American jet was forced to land on China's Hainan Island.

I had totally forgotten about my prediction until the newscast gave the details. Although the incident was very sad, it was interesting to note that my prediction was accurate even to the day. I did see three jets, but only two countries were involved-- China and the United States. The only discrepancy was Taiwan was not in the conflict.

Chapter IV

Holiday Reflections

My father Michael Novak

A Father's Day Hello

It was an overcast day that Father's Day in June of 2012. Though it hadn't rained all day, the sky looked somewhat threatening. My son Marc came over about 8:00 p.m. and asked if I wanted to go outside on the deck. I replied, "Let's take a walk down the street instead." He agreed, but as we started to walk, he suggested we go around the block. I hesitated at first because I did not want to go very far, but went anyway.

Unfortunately, when we got half way around the block it started to pour down rain. I didn't have a jacket, but at least my straw hat offered some protection for my head. I soon started yelling because my clothes were getting quite wet and the wind was very strong. All at once a lady came out and asked if we wanted garbage bags to use as cover ups. We both accepted her offer, but Marc ran home to get the van instead, while I scootered inside her garage and sat there as she covered me with large black garbage bags.

I thanked her and asked for her name. ''My name is Faith Nowakowski'', she replied. It startled me to hear the name Nowakowski because immediately my father's name, Michael Novak, came to mind. Those two last names were too close to dismiss.

Was it meant that we took a walk around the block so we could meet Faith Nowakowski on Father's Day? If we only walked down the street, we would have been home before it had rained. Meeting a woman with the last name, Nowakowski, was amazingly close to Novak, my maiden name and my Dad's last name. Was this a way for my father to say 'hello' to me on his special day? I believe he was also telling me to keep the 'Faith' in my life.

The Christmas Concert

During the holiday season in 1997, I attended a beautiful Christmas concert at Troy Baptist Church. The sights and sounds were really exciting. When the choir sang songs with words like Jesus, Immanuel, and Hallelujah, I felt like rising up and singing with my hands held high. A few times I bowed my head and went into instant meditation and prayer. With this feeling of exultation came a need to tape record the music, so I began to record the first half of the concert.

I went to the lobby to listen to the tape during the intermission. To my dismay, none of the music was recorded. This surprised me because it worked properly before the concert. It seemed as though most of the tape had been erased. I said, "Testing, one, two, three." and rewound it to hear my voice. Instead, I heard my boss' voice say, "This is Bob, testing, one, two, three." My voice had not recorded, or so I thought. Later that evening when I played the tape, I heard my voice clearly.

Earlier that evening I had contemplated going to my office after the concert to get my payroll check. Even though my office was a couple of miles away, I had hesitated because it was late and I had to get up early the next day. Nevertheless, I decided to go there anyway. I left the concert fifteen minutes early at 9:45 p.m. and arrived at my office 10:00 p.m. Upon opening the door, I noticed the Christmas lights on the plant were still on... This was a fire hazard.

As I analyzed the events of the last two days, I saw everything fall into place. My sister, Diane, had stopped by to see me at the office where she rarely visited. She had suggested putting lights on the plant. Had she not made this suggestion, I probably would not have strung the lights in the first place.

I believe Spirit beckoned to me through the tape to return to my office that evening to avert the possibility of a fire happening. Certainly, if the tape had recorded the concert, I would never have rewound it and tested it. Bob's voice was only on that part of the tape. Why did I rewind it to his voice? This was a clue from Spirit to get back to the office to avert a fire. If my paycheck had come two days earlier as it usually does, I would not have needed to visit my office that evening. I believe the real or spiritual reason to go back to the office was to shut off the Christmas lights; the physical reason was to get my paycheck.

The Christmas Bow

One Christmas season while shopping at a store in Sterling Heights, Michigan, I purchased a small beautiful gold basket with an angel inside. Unfortunately, the next day, the bow on the basket handle had fallen off. I looked everywhere but was unable to find it. When I went back to the store, a replacement bow was not available.

After a week had passed, I went shopping at the same store in Waterford located forty miles from the other store. To my surprise, I discovered the 'special bow' on a shelf by itself among merchandise not related to Christmas. I asked the store clerk if I could purchase the bow. She said I could have it free of charge.

Did my guardian angel make sure I would find the bow at another store when I needed it? My feeling was that finding that same bow would normally be slim to none-- this was a miracle.

Fireplace Embers

One day upon returning home from a shopping spree, I noticed the remnants of a fire Marc had set in my fireplace. The flames dwindling to embers was a disappointing scene. It would have been nice to relax in front of the fireplace with a glass of wine. Immediately, I said ''I wish the fire would come alive again.''

Upon leaving the room to go to the bathroom, I was gone only a few minutes when Marc exclaimed, ''Mom, there are flames that suddenly appeared in the fireplace, and I didn't add any more wood to reignite it.

Why did the flames appear just when I asked for them- -not five minutes earlier or five minutes later? The flames lasted approximately thirty minutes. Most people would think of this occurrence as a coincidence; but because there are no coincidences, my request being granted was a miracle in the happening.

My Wishes Granted

In the past several years I have paid attention to quite a few names, numbers, words and circumstances that have crossed my path. Living a spiritual life has brought me both good and challenging situations. I believe many of my wishes comes true because I am in a state called cosmic consciousness which means every physical event has a spiritual cause.

1. While working as a receptionist at a temporary job assignment, someone walked in and asked me to call 911. I made the call stating that a young girl had parked in a no parking zone next to our building; thus, a car drove down the street and crashed into her parked car. When the police arrived, they came inside and described what had happened--luckily the girl wasn't injured. I was still curious about this situation, so I felt a need to go outside. As I left the building, I looked down and saw a pencil sharpener... this was what I had wished for a few minutes before. It was unusual that I had to deal with this accident to find a simple thing as a pencil sharpener.

2. One day while on my scooter in my small kitchen, I accidentally drove into the cupboard and hit my big toe. It was very painful and thought my bone was

broken. A couple days before, I spoke of getting new tennis shoes because my shoes were too small. Was this meant to happen so I would be unable to wear the shoes because of the pain, and be forced to buy new shoes? I also said that I hadn't gone anywhere in the car for quite a while. Did cosmic forces hear my request so I could be driven to 'Patients First' to get x-rays? Even though I had to suffer, this was a chance to get out. This story, although simple, is an example why everything that happens in the physical has another real meaning which is of Spirit.

3. When I first moved to a condominium in Sterling Heights, I had mixed feelings about living upstairs and being in a somewhat remote location at the end of the complex. Though I enjoyed being near the woods and pond, I didn't have a chance to meet many people. One afternoon, I was wishing to meet another neighbor besides the couple next door. Within a few minutes my doorbell rang--As I opened the door, a man introduced himself as my neighbor. He explained that he had my package sent to him by mistake and was returning it to me. He said ''If you need anything, just let me know.'' He also gave me the location of his condo which was very close to mine. I replied ''Thank you, it was nice meeting you.'' My wish was granted.

4. Another time, Laurel, and Marc had mentioned they were going to a restaurant when they left my house. I added, "Sometimes I get a small magazine that has coupons for nearby restaurants." Within three minutes, Laurel went to the mailbox and pulled out one of those small magazines. I was astonished to see this mail right after I had mentioned it. I believe it was already known ahead of time that I would be asking

for this magazine with restaurant coupons. They both were happy to find the coupon they wanted.

5. I was feeling lonely between Christmas and New Year's Eve 2013. I felt like some of my friends were abandoning me. Sometimes I would call them but they didn't call me back when I hoped to talk with them; and I wished that they would call me more often. From January 1st through the 3rd, I received eight phone calls from my lady friends. This was another way the Universe granted my wish.

Apple Pies

In September 2009, Laurel and I visited Michigan. Steven, a good friend of the family, was gracious enough to share his house with us for ten days. During this time, my father, Michael Novak, seemed to be around me once again. I believe our deceased relatives make their presence known when we least expect it.

This time having three apple pies in my midst made me think of daddy. First, I ordered a healthy apple pie from Life Smart Foods store. Second, the dessert at Laurel's family dinner party was an apple pie. Third, Steven's father baked an apple pie. My dad loved the apple pies that I used to bake for my parents.

Did these three pies appear in sequence for a reason? Was my dad communicating in this way so I would think of him? What resonated with me the most was that Steven's father had baked the pie himself. How often do men make apple pies? When the word father was mentioned, my dad immediately came to mind. Interestingly, Steven's house is located on Applewood Drive in Warren, Michigan.

Chapter V

Family and Friends

My Mother Ruth and I

My granddaughter Jennifer's Communion

My Mother Ruth

''I can't think about that right now, if I do, I'll go crazy. I'll think about that tomorrow... After all tomorrow is another day.'' These words were spoken by Katie Scarlett O'Hara from the 1939 Oscar winning movie ''Gone with the Wind.'' This was my mother Ruth's favorite movie. She would also often say ''I'll think about that tomorrow.''

My mother, Ruth Gillespie Novak, made her transition in April 2003 after suffering from dementia and kidney cancer. Before she left this earth, she lived in my sister Diane's home for about a year. Unfortunately at age 81, she never fully recovered from hip surgery. My sister and her family took good care of her with the help of home care aides. I also spent the night at Diane's home a few days a week, lending a helping hand until mom's demise at 82 years old.

I believe my mother and I were soul mates because we went to the same elementary and high school. We both married men named Michael, who were born in February. We each had two children. We both had back injuries, had fallen a few times and could not walk well. Lastly, we were easy-going individuals with the same numerology Life Path of 4.

My mother was a wonderful person and I dearly miss her. After she passed, I did hear her call my name one night as I laid in bed. She used to call me in the same way to get up for work when I spent the night in Waterford.

Since 2011, I have received messages from other deceased relatives. I have not heard from my mother except when she called me as stated above. Consequently, on June 29, 2012, I said "Mom, I haven't heard from you in a while--please contact me." During the next week, I felt these hidden messages came from my mother.

1. On June 30, while at a friend's party, the speaker had a book called 'Take Me To Truth' laying on the table. When I looked down at the book, the letter 'T' was not seen because of the angle of my view... Instead the title 'Take Me To Ruth' appeared to me.

2. The next day, I looked in my cookbook and just happened to turn to the page titled 'Ruth's Noodle Pudding'. My mom often made a similar dish.

3. On July 2, I watched a movie 'Elephant Walk' starring Elizabeth Taylor in which her name just happened to be Ruth.

4. The next day, I saw 'Ruth to the Rescue' on the local news--she helps people solve various challenges. The movie star, Ruth Hussey's name appeared on television advertising her upcoming movie.

It was very refreshing to know my mother heard me call her. As with my other deceased relatives, we understand that even though we don't see them they are still around us. I feel my mother is happy residing in heaven, and hope to see her and my father again someday.

Aunt Helen

In April 2012, I returned home one evening to discover a surprising message left on my answering machine: ''Yes Michele, this is Aunt Helen. I want to RSVP, but I want to know exactly where the church is because I have no idea. I'll either call you or you'll have to call me back if you don't mind. Have a nice evening.''

I listened to this message a few times, because I knew that I didn't have an 'Aunt Helen'. The only Aunt Helen I knew was a relative of my best friend, Suzanne, but my granddaughter, Jennifer, was having her First Communion at a church in Sterling Heights at the end of the month. It could have been an RSVP from someone I didn't know.

The following day I called 'Aunt Helen' at the number found on my caller ID. When she answered, I responded "This is Michele" and gave her directions to the church. Thinking this was Theresa's aunt, I questioned her..."I don't have an Aunt Helen. Did Theresa give you my number for directions to the church?" ''No'', she replied, suddenly realizing she had misdialed. Her niece, also named Michele, had the same number as mine but a different area code.

My curiosity prompted me to call her niece Michele who explained that her daughter was also making her First Communion at a church near Birmingham, Michigan.

There was the obvious reason for the original call from 'Aunt Helen'.

While it was extraordinary that both of us spelled our names with only one *L*, and had the identical phone number except for the area code, I wondered about the spiritual reason behind this call. Could Suzanne's deceased Aunt Helen have been talking to me? We were quite close when she was alive because I knew her daughter, Gloria, in elementary school, and sat next to her in Spanish class. I met her deceased son, Gregory, in high school, whom I often saw at a mutual friend's home. I met her niece, Suzanne, when I was 19 years old, and we are still close friends. Since I've known Helen's family for nearly 50 years, I believe we are a soul group, brought together on earth to enjoy a loving relationship as friends.

An Abscess Obsession

I moved back to Michigan from Tallahassee, Florida in July, 2011. My son Marc had found me a foreclosed house in Warren, Michigan. After some remodeling, it blossomed into a beautiful home and I have enjoyed compliments given by friends and family.

Since moving back, I had not been to the dentist for about a year, so I decided to get a checkup and teeth cleaning. The dental hygienist checked my gums and x-rayed my back teeth. She then proceeded to clean my teeth. While using a sharp instrument, she touched between my front teeth causing a filling to fall out. Before she went any further, the dentist came in to examine the tooth and asked her to take another x-ray. She was unable to complete my cleaning because we ran out of time.

After my son Michael lifted me onto the scooter, we went to the lobby and waited for my results. Soon the hygienist told my son that I had an abscess in that front tooth and suggested that I get a root canal as soon as possible. I wasn't experiencing pain, so I didn't begin a root canal until almost three months later.

Within a month, I began to research information on root canals online which revealed that root canals can be dangerous. In light of that, I decided to go to another dentist for a second opinion. At first, the second dentist had encouraged me to get an implant. I had no interest in this because it would cost about $4,000. She added, ''As for a root canal, since there is only one canal, it shouldn't pose a health threat.'' Thinking she was correct with her assessment, I went to see an endodontist, who is a root canal specialist. He explained the procedure saying that root canals can sometimes fail. If that occurs, surgery might be necessary. I agreed to begin the root canal feeling it necessary to begin treatment since I had waited so long.

In the meantime, I had information sent through e-mail about root canals, which said to avoid them because there is a chance the bacteria will go throughout your body.

This uncertainty began to cause me concern. ''What would another option be?'' I thought. I then went to a third dentist for other options. He said I could get an implant or a fixed bridge. My decision was to get the bridge. He also gave me a prescription for penicillin that I did not get filled for about two weeks. I began taking the penicillin because I started feeling ill with ear and headaches and a fever of 99 degrees, though I'm not a big fan of antibiotics, which affect the intestinal flora.

Two weeks later, I returned to the dentist to start the fixed bridge. To my dismay, he wanted me to take more medication (four capsules of an antibiotic). I did not want to take this medication, but forced myself to take one, dissolving it in my mouth. It was very strong, and knew my bladder would become agitated if I were to take any more pills. I did not want to engage with this treatment protocol, so we left immediately. After going to three dentists, and one endodontist, this became a real fiasco to say the least. This began to be a real abscess obsession.

Thank God, soon after the spiritual realm came to my rescue. Knowing that they would be there for me should never be questioned because by living pure spirit so much that I ask for comes to me within a short time.

I felt guided to go back to my dentist from the past, Dr. Michael Harris. One reason I hesitated to go back to him initially was because he was out of network with my insurance. Also, his office was a little further away than the other dentists. I was led to call him anyway because I know my deceased parents, who have always been there for me while alive, were helping me from the other side. I believe they had nudged me to contact Dr. Harris because besides being an excellent dentist his first name is Michael and his billing specialist is Ruth. My father's name was Michael and my mother, Ruth. My father and Dr. Harris's father were also friends... maybe they were talking in Heaven.

My experience at Arch Dental was wonderful. The dentist and his staff treated me like royalty. They did an excellent job on my fixed bridge which did involve pulling the tooth and they didn't require me to consume prescription drugs.

In the midst of all this chaos and before the tooth extraction, Dr. Cody, who's a holistic doctor, happened to call me. I explained that I was not feeling well and believed the abscess could have traveled through my bloodstream. He said his therapy to raise my vibration would help. My second cousin, Brian Parenteau, whom I had just met, also gave me three ozone treatments that were beneficial.

My friend, Suzanne, cited an incident of a man who lost his life from waiting too long to treat an abscess tooth, and consequently developed sepsis. I had also read about endocarditis (inflammation of the inner layer of the heart) which comes from tooth abscesses. This condition can affect the heart valve with symptoms including fever, breathing difficulties, neck and head pains-- all of which I had been experiencing. In the middle of the night I awoke with a really strange feeling going up and down my body. I asked God to keep me alive for my sons' and granddaughter's sake.

It was a blessing in disguise that the hygienist caused my filling to come out, and x-rayed my front teeth to discover there was an abscess tooth. I did not know about the dangers of a tooth abscess affecting your body. Consequently, not having any pain, I took my time getting it treated. Did I go to the dentist who gave me the strong medication for a reason? Had he not given me penicillin on my first visit, my life might have been in danger.

Other health practitioners gave me heart supplements and essential oils that eased my discomfort. The fact that Dr. Cody gave me distant vibrational therapy proved beneficial. It was great to read information about root canals sent through e-mail. All these therapies and information came to me at the exact time I needed them.

It really caught my eye when letters from a vitamin bottle label and my Doctor's name, spelled the word 'valve'. Was this a way Spirit let me know that my heart valve was affected?

If we look at my cousin's last name which is Parenteau, we see the word parent. It seems like this was a clue that my parents were there to help me make the right decisions during this traumatic event.

Joy And Sorrow

The death of my grandmother Julia on June 18, 1997, and birth of my great niece were both memorable events in my life. Never before have I felt such anguish and so much joy at the same time. One day my grief stricken heart felt weak with the news of my grandmother's death only to feel strong again on the next day with the birth of my new greatniece. Spiritually speaking, I do not believe in the concept of birth and death, but physically I felt the impact.

When my great niece, Brooke Elizabeth Wylin was born on June 19, 1997 at 10:20 p.m., an interesting spiritual happening took place. That day, my mother, sister and I had spent many hours waiting at the hospital hoping that we would all be there when the baby was being born. Since this was my niece Lisa's first child, her labor seemed like it would never end, so they decided to induce labor. We asked the nurse approximately how much longer before she would deliver and she replied, "It will be several more hours." Knowing this, I decided to go home, and my sister Diane drove our mother home.

Diane was only gone about an hour, so when she arrived back at the hospital, Lisa had already given birth to a little girl. Grandma Diane was very upset that she was gone right at the time of the birth. Of course, she so wanted to be there, but would not have been allowed in the birthing room anyway.

Did this happen for a reason? If grandma Diane had to sit out in the lobby during the birth of her first grandchild, she would have felt unhappy and left out. The fact that she wasn't there was by far a much easier pill to swallow.

Birth and death seem to be similar in that when you are born you go from darkness to light. Also during the change called death, you are in darkness and you see light at the tunnel's end as described in a near-death experience. In both cases you are greeted by loved ones to help with the transition.

Michaels in My Life

Through the years I have had many Michaels in my life. My family members include my father, ex-husband, my son, my nephew, and my ex-husband's nephew. Besides my family, many other Michaels have crossed my path and touched my life in a positive way.

In 1994, during my bout with breast cancer, a friend recommended an oncologist with the first name Michael. He was a good doctor who was very caring and showed exceptional concern for my well-being. We had read that his treatment plan for me would give the best results.

In 2007, three more Michaels including St. Michael's church, came into my life during the year I lived at a retirement facility in Shelby Township, Michigan. Michael Walsh would help me with chores and often drove me to appointments. Almost every day we would go around the complex while enjoying the beautiful woods. We also participated in various social activities together.

I contacted St. Michael's church to ask if they would provide a volunteer to assist me with cooking. I was delighted when they sent a lovely lady to help me in the kitchen for about four months.

During that same year, Michael Ellegion lived with me for two weeks. He was a well-known channel, UFO researcher and author of the book "Prepare for the Landings". At the time, he lived in Arizona and was visiting Michigan to participate in various speaking engagements.

Initially, Michael stayed with my friend Bob and his roommates but had to move out due to a lack of space in the house. Bob asked if I would be willing to allow him to stay with me for the remainder of his time here. I was glad to accommodate him after Bob reassured me that Michael was trustworthy and would give me a free 90 minute Transformational Channeled Reading in exchange for him staying with me.

During the reading, Michael direct voice channeled Ashtar and a female who were both Cosmic Light beings and members of the Galactic Federation of Light. I received an insight into the future, and other good advice. He also did a Cosmic Color meditation and a Chakra Clearing session. He stated that if someone else wanted a session, to contact him at 206-235-8402. His website is MichaelEllegion.com and his email address is **Vortexnetwork@hotmail.com**.

Originally, Michael Ellegion was trained as a young child through the Edgar Cayce method of channeling by his father who was a professional stage hypnotist. He also had physical contact and joyous etheric visitations of these higher human appearing space beings while growing up, as well as protecting him and saving his life many times.

I believe it was meant that Michael and I connect because I moved here from my condo near the time he needed accommodations. Plus the fact that my departed father and mother still seem to be around bringing another

Michael to me. If we look at Michael's phone number, the numbers 225 are the same as my father's birthday February 25. Michael's birthday is September 20 or 9-20 and my father's Life path is 9. My mother was born in 1920 which corresponds to the day Michael was born. We also see 8 and 4. The 8 is my Attitude number and 4 is my Life Path number (See Numerology story).

When my family and I arrived at the retirement facility, we looked for a one-bedroom apartment. Though we found a nice one on the second floor, we soon realized it didn't have a dishwasher. Upon looking further, we found a two-bedroom on the first floor with a dishwasher. It was a nice place that had a beautiful view of the woods and a gazebo nearby.

If I didn't have a two-bedroom apartment, Michael would not have been comfortable living there with me. He was fortunate to have his own bedroom with full bathroom and closets. Also, I happened to have a small table in his bedroom which he used when people came over for channelings. It was also convenient for them to enter through my French doors from the back of the complex instead of the main lobby.

While at Bob's monthly party, I felt Michael was my son in another lifetime. My current son is named Michael; so it's feasible that I had a son at another time with the same name.

It was a pleasure having Michael live with me those two weeks. He expressed that in order to connect with him, a person must be at least 200 on the ' Harmonic Vibrational Scale' as well as have 51% of negative accumulated karma out of the way.

The next three Michaels had included my Dentist, my Cardiologist and a Holistic Doctor. Their advice and treatments have been helpful for my well being.

Another Michael, whom I have known for about three years, is my scooter repairman. At times he really saved the day when the scooter I ride required immediate attention. I appreciated his assistance during my time of need.

There are 8 Michaels in this story, including a church. If we add 5 relatives, the grand total is 13 Michaels. Bless all of these Michaels who have helped me in some capacity. I am grateful that the Universe brought them into my life!

Jim's Spiritual Awakening

My niece Lisa's husband Jim and I have had a good rapport for many years. He has been there to help me and my family many times in the past.

In December 26, 2009, he lost his brother Mark to colon cancer. Mark had suffered five years before his transition. Jim was devastated to lose his brother at the age of 50.

At his brother's burial, he saw a vision of Mark saying "Take care of yourself--don't be the next one."

Now Jim is proud to say he walks three miles a day and has quit his bad habits of drinking alcohol and smoking cigarettes and eats much healthier. Jim says he feels better because of these changes. He also quit his real estate job and only works for Chrysler Corporation. Working less hours enables Jim to participate in school activities with his two children. Also, the four of them can enjoy more outings together as a family.

Even though Jim was upset about his brother, in the physical realm, passing on...In a spiritual way, something good came from something bad.

Parallel Lives

In 1998, while living in Greenville, I contacted my temporary agency and expressed to the agent that I had just returned from visiting Michigan for Easter and wondered if there were any job assignments for me. Hearing that I was from Michigan, she commented that she was from Warren, Michigan and lived on Mound Road, about five miles from where I used to live.

She explained that Bob Jones University in South Carolina was the college she had attended and the place where she met her husband. I said I had met a man by the same name in Greenville with the same circumstances. We were amazed that her husband was the same person that I knew. Even though I didn't know her very well, spiritually there seemed to be a connection. I assumed we were soul mates living parallel lives on the Earth whereby experiencing the same circumstances. I feel we were meant to reunite by divine arrangement.

Recently, my daughter-in-law Laurel had told me that she also knows another married couple with the same names as my friends. This seemed possible because Laurel and I are soul mates having parallel lives. For example, one time I had a party and had very few people attend because of last minute cancellations. She also had a party during the same time and had poor attendance because most of the guests canceled at the last minute.

My sister, Diane, and I have also noticed on several occasions that we are on the same path at the same time. For instance, she will mention that she is getting her hair cut tomorrow and I am also getting my haircut tomorrow. Another time, she explained that she wasn't sure about putting a name in a story in a newsletter while in Florida. I also wasn't sure about putting a name in a story for this book.

Before coming to live on earth, we are able to choose the souls that are best suited for us during each lifetime. We are usually comfortable coming back with the same soul group each time to deal with unfinished business. This is why we sometimes feel that we have known someone for a long time even though we had never met them before. Most of us have been on a journey here on earth that has lasted hundreds or perhaps thousands of years.

The Broken Necklace

One afternoon, I went to see my neurologist. While sitting in the lobby, I had broken my necklace. Laurel began trying to fix it, but had a difficult time reattaching the two pieces of the broken chain. I said, "You need a pair of tweezers." All at once a lady sitting in back of us said, "There are tweezers on the table next to you." Laurel took them and proceeded to repair my necklace. I thought this was a miracle because I've never heard of tweezers being in a doctor's waiting room.

Chapter VI

Rescued

Helpful Headlights

On a 1999 winter evening in Greenville, I decided to go to the drugstore. For some reason, I decided to leave my handbag at home, only taking my change purse and keys. When I reached the drug store, my change purse was gone. I went into the store anyway without any money. I returned to the apartment, but was unable to find my change purse.

I went down to the parking lot to recheck my car and my son's car to see if the purse had fallen on the ground or possibly in the parking lot. As I walked near the area where I had originally parked, two cars came by. One car drove by, but the other pulled into the parking space next to where I was standing, its headlights shining directly on my change purse laying on the ground. It was my neighbor's car, whom I believe was meant to come home at the exact time I needed his headlights.

I encountered more helpful headlights the next night when I went outside to take out the garbage. I decided to check my car tire because it appeared to be somewhat low earlier. It was dark and difficult to see, but then a car drove by right when I was looking down at the tire. Those headlights enabled me to see that the tire was indeed low, but I could wait to drive to the gas station to fill it with air the next day.

I wondered about the real reason I left my handbag at home. I believe this was a way the Universe revealed that I would be helped, no matter what. If I had taken my handbag, it wouldn't have fallen, and none of this would have happened. I know that if the headlights did not provide light to see the change purse, there was a good chance it would have been stolen the next day.

In the tire scenario, it was better to learn the condition of the tire that evening. If it was flat, I could immediately call road service to repair the tire. Another lesson I learned from both situations was to have a flashlight available to use at night when visibility is poor.

Help on the Road

One rainy evening, I was a judge at a speech and debate tournament affiliated with my son's speech program at his high school in South Carolina. It was very rewarding to participate in this tournament.

As I left that night, driving out of the parking lot to the main road, visibility was very poor. I had a desire for yogurt, so I began looking for a TCBY yogurt store. I got sidetracked, however, when noticing my bank on the left side of the street. The idea of getting cash at the drive through ATM machine sounded great; so I went through the drive through and inserted my ATM card as usual. Unfortunately, it took me a little longer to answer the final questions because reaching from my car on a rainy evening was a bit awkward. Consequently, the machine had swallowed my card! I was upset, but when returning the next day to pick up my card, I understood why this had happened.

After getting my card, I drove out of the bank parking lot, and found myself on a side street waiting at a trafficlight. I was still in the mood for yogurt, but wasn't sure where TCBY was located... so turning right or left was the big question. Then I noticed a van in front of me with 227 as part of the license plate number. Feeling lost, it seemed as though this van crossed my path for a reason. I felt whatever direction the van turned must be the right way to TCBY since these numbers appear in my life so often. The van turned left and all at once my hand hit the turn signal with a downward motion to also turn left.

The van went another way, but I kept driving and something told me to put on my left turn signal again. I turned into an unfamiliar bank parking lot. As I drove through the parking lot, lo and behold the TCBY Yogurt store was directly in front of me.

Did I lose the ATM card for a reason? By losing the card it forced me to go back the next day and realize that I would get help locating the Yogurt store during the day when visibility was much better. Was the van also there to assist me because I paid attention to the familiar numbers? I felt as though my guardian angel or an unknown force was there to help me drive my car. This seemed apparent when I turned left at the unfamiliar bank parking lot right in front of TCBY. Throughout this event, I felt like I was in the twilight zone.

A Stranger Guides My Way

It was a snowy evening in December when I ventured out to a Christmas party to be the entertainment. As I drove through an unfamiliar, exclusive neighborhood, the darkness made seeing the street names and house numbers very difficult. As I turned back from making a wrong turn, I noticed a man walking out of his driveway waving his arms motioning for me to pull into the driveway.

As I stopped the car, he said ''I was worried that you had gotten lost.'' Expecting this to be my destination, I asked him to help carry some of my bags. He responded by asking if I was Marion. We both realized that this was a clear case of mistaken identity. I said that I was looking for the Stuart's house. He knew exactly where they lived down the street.

The timing was perfect. Had I been a few minutes earlier or later we would not have connected. Furthermore, the identity of the car and the person that he was expecting seemed to be unknown. Why was I chosen to be flagged down? Was it also meant that he knew where the Stuart's lived so he could direct me there because I was lost. This was surely a miracle.

Driving Alone

Before Marc and I moved to South Carolina in February, 1998, we had gone to Georgia and South Carolina to evaluate what location would best suit our way of living. This trip took place in January of 1998. Marc wanted to drive alone in early February to check out the area once more. Of course, I was against the idea so I prayed for guidance.

We received three insurance advertisements for Accidental Death due to injury in the mail the next day. I believe this was a warning from the Universe to not let him go because of possible danger. My son immediately hugged me and said "Mom, I'm not going to go-- this must be a sign."

Why did those advertisements arrive at the exact time we needed to know this? The clue was a written notice sent through the mail.

Rescued At Home

It was a pleasant Fall morning in October 2011 when I arose at 8:00 a.m. As I sat up in bed, I lost my balance and fell straight back...one might compare this happening to a turtle. If you've seen a turtle fall on its back, it has a difficult time turning over. Well, it was also very difficult for me, so going down to the floor seemed like the only option. My legs were already on the floor, so it was easy to crawl down.

As I have MS, I then tried to stand up by my scooter but failed. After a few more times of trying to anchor my right foot on the ground and hoist myself up, I still couldn't get up. After several more tries, I decided to call my health care aide. She said she would come over, so I began crawling on the wood floor to reach the front door, but my knees became sore and couldn't continue. I then called her back to cancel.

My next call was to 911. To my surprise, however, someone answered the call from Tallahassee, Florida where I used to live because I was still registered in that area. I explained the situation that I now live in Michigan so he said to try the call again. My phone call temporarily did not go through, so I used the cell phone to contact Warren, Michigan where I reside. Within twenty minutes, the fire department arrived but couldn't get in because both doors were bolted. I gave them the French door code to no avail because it was securely locked.

I then heard footsteps on my roof. They finally gained entry through an open bedroom window which was probably left open when my ex- roommate had put in an air conditioner.

Did this happen for a reason? If this did not happen, I would not have known that I was still in Tallahassee's emergency system. This was very important because my emergency device that I wore around my neck would have gone to Tallahassee instead of Michigan. Thus, If I would have fallen somewhere else in the house without a telephone, this would have complicated getting a quick response. Also I felt that it was meant that the window was left open upstairs allowing them to enter the house. I knew I was being taken care of by the Universe in a timely fashion.

Stairway Mishap

On October 12th of 2005, I made an appointment to see my health practitioner. I lived in a condo located on the second floor. I was diagnosed with Multiple Sclerosis in 2004 so my legs did not always cooperate with me.

As I left to go to the appointment and began walking down the stairs, the soles of my black shoes began to stick on the stairway carpet. Consequently, I fell because my left leg had gotten stuck. I grabbed the left railing only-- there was no railing on the right side to grasp. Terrified, I started calling loudly ''God -- Angels please help me.'' I suddenly let go of the left railing and managed to sit on the stairs and pulled my left leg, slowly straightening it. Luckily, I was halfway down the stairs, so I was able to slide down the rest of the way in a sitting position.

Amazingly enough, two people came right at the time this happened. The UPS delivery man came to the door, and my friend Suzanne dropped over unexpectedly to clean my home. If for some reason I was unable to get down the stairs myself, someone would have been there to assist me.

I believe God heard my call for help. Being so upset at that moment and afraid of falling, it didn't occur to me to sit down. Did divine intervention play a role and give me the message to sit down? The fact that two people were there to help me was truly incredible. Soon after, we purchased a chairlift, so this mishap would not occur again.

A Dilemma Resolved

My Power Chair had been my way to get around town in Tallahassee, Florida. It was fun going to different stores; and seeing sights and hearing sounds in a different way from driving a car.

One Saturday afternoon, I scootered to a small clothing shop that also has some nice matching jewelry. After shopping, I started to go to my son's house a few streets away. My mind changed when I noticed my scooter was running out of power, so I got back on the street and headed home. I had to keep turning the scooter on and off so it wouldn't lose power. I was concerned whether or not I would get home safely because it moved very slow. About halfway there, a lady called out to see if I could get around her car. When I tried to explain that my scooter was almost out of power, she didn't seem to understand; so she proceeded to park on the sidewalk right in front of me. Lately, she had been parking on the sidewalk which blocked my path.

I called my son on the cell phone and he soon came to my aid. My son asked her to move; she did so, and apologized for parking there. Her gentleman friend said she parks there to avoid the cars on the street that have to pass by her. Later my son came by and explained to them there is an ordinance to prohibit anyone from parking on the sidewalk. She said it wouldn't happen again.

We went back, showed them the ordinance papers, and took pictures of the car to assure that this would never happen again.

This incident happened for a reason. If my scooter had not lost almost all the power, I would not have been able to speak to her about not parking on the sidewalk. Unfortunately, her car had been in my way for the past two or three months, but we had not asked her to move until now. We now could enforce this issue with proof. This meeting was not a coincidence, it happened in divine order.

The Right Repair

Just before Christmas 2010, I contacted the scooter repairman, Steve, and asked him to replace my armrests because they were worn out. I had become concerned because I had not heard from him in almost a month. I called him back on January 16 and left a message. He called me back about 11:00 a.m. the next day, apologized and explained he had some difficulty getting the correct part. I then expressed the fact that the lever that moves the scooter had lost a screw.

I hung up the phone and put it on charger in the bedroom. I then went towards the living room with only one screw remaining, hoping the scooter would still work okay. I got as far as the fireplace when the other screw also fell off. Thus, it would not move because the lever had fallen off. A feeling of despair and helplessness engulfed my being, but I soon realized my scooter had landed right next to another phone. Steve's phone number was still on my caller ID, because he had called me back about 15 minutes before I had gotten stuck. This enabled me to call him back and explain what had just happened. He said he would soon come back to replace the screw.

I called my son Marc to rescue me. He came over and wheeled my walker to me so I could walk to my other scooter which was close by. Unfortunately, I cannot walk very far.

The fact that my scooter landed right next to the phone allowing me to call Steve and Marc immediately. It was fortunate that my son Marc was available to come to my aid. Was it meant that the scooter stalled in a perfect location in the house so I could walk a short distance to the other scooter? If it had stalled in my small kitchen, bathroom, hallway, or walk -in closet, we would have had to call the fire department for assistance. I believe Universal forces came through to help me with this situation.

A Chance Encounter

One summer night, a girlfriend and I went to a night-club to dance. While standing near the bar, I noticed a handsome man staring at me. He approached me and said, "I danced with you at Jack's not long ago-- you were very shy". I gave him a puzzled look, knowing I had never met him. Ralph continued, "I thought I would never see you again". My first thought was that he was handing me a line. However, I was curious to know more about him.

After dancing and more conversation, we parted for a short time, then reconnected. When saying our good-byes, another stranger approached; He said, "You look very familiar to me". Ralph replied, "See I told you". Immediately, I felt that this was a confirmation of what Ralph had said earlier... that he was telling the truth.

On our first date, Ralph spoke of Mary, my look-a-like. They had danced only twice before she announced that she had to leave. Instead, she kept staring at him and wouldn't talk or dance with anyone else-- then suddenly vanished.

We continued to date. One month after Ralph's divorce was final, I realized why we had connected. He had just received devastating news from his ex-wife. She was romantically involved with their son's friend's father--

someone they had both known for twenty years. During his despair, I spent the evening comforting him. He said, "God sent you to me, the timing was so right".

If Mary hadn't made such an impact on Ralph, he might not have connected with me. Was this a divine arrangement that compelled us to meet? Was the Universe calling me through Mary to help Ralph?

Chapter VII

Memories

A Civil War Soldier

I believe we all have existed before in another physical body, known as reincarnation. Each soul has its own personality with all the human emotions. The soul is involved in every decision we make in our physical life. We can ask our soul for help to heal our emotional and physical body. In order for each soul to grow, many lifetimes provide many opportunities.

One day in 1998 while living in Greenville, I asked Spirit to give me information about a past life. Well, the information came to me within a couple days. As I stood in the kitchen, a strange noise came from the apartment above us. Strangely enough, it sounded familiar, possibly soldiers playing drums on the battlefield. Physically, someone was probably using a clothes dryer, but spiritually this could have stirred up a memory from a war. I have always been interested in the Civil War and thought I could have been a soldier in that war during in a past life because in a dream a cannon appeared in the street.

On our honeymoon, we went to Gettysburg, Pennsylvania, where the battle of Gettysburg was fought. I felt such a connection with that town, so we went back there on another vacation to tour the battlefield.

The next day I went to the local library because I was very anxious to learn more about the Civil War. My first stop before the library, however, was to register for another temporary agency. While in the lobby, I had to look up a telephone number. As I reached under the table to get a phone book, I noticed a gold button on the floor. This button had an emblem on it similar to one found on an army uniform. Was this a message?

I found a book at the library on the Civil War. For some reason one soldier's name really struck a cord with me. His name was John Caldwell McLemore, a Confederate soldier who died of a head injury in Manassas (Bull Run) Virginia. I have found many similarities between Colonel McLemore and myself.

1. We both have dark-hair and attractive features.

2. I lived on Caldwell Street in Detroit while growing up.

3. I have had three head injuries in my life.

4. Compare the letters in the name John Caldwell McLemore to Michele Novak Stemmer. Michele has Mcle , Novak has o and Stemmer has m--and re.

5. Many people have been in my life with 'Mc' and 'more' in their names.

6. Noticed words Manassas, Virginia on my credit card bill.

7. Colonel McLemore was ranked under Major Thomas McCreary. My former boss had the last name McCready with only one letter different. He also lived on South Boulevard.

It's difficult to explain why I feel that I was John Caldwell McLemore in another lifetime. It seems that Spirit once again has given me this information to ponder.

I have also believed that I was either related to General Robert E. Lee, of the Confederacy or had some connection to him at another time because I have met a few men named Robert Lee.

Richard Taylor

While living in South Carolina, another past life had come to my attention. I felt that I was Richard Taylor, the father of PresIdent Zachary Taylor. In 1996 my son Marc revealed that he was very interested in politics and wanted to be president someday. I noticed that there is an arc in Zachary and an arc in Marc's name. Also, Marc resembles Zachary Taylor, and they both have dark hair and brown eyes. Intuitively it came to me that he could have been Zachary Taylor in another lifetime.

I went to a local bookstore and borrowed a book about Richard Taylor so I could put more of the puzzle pieces together. The book stated that he attended William and Mary College in Williamsburg, Virginia. While vacationing there, I had also visited the college. I really loved Williamsburg because it was historic and beautiful. He attended Harvard-- Marc said he also wanted to attend Harvard. Colonel Taylor like John Caldwell McLemore (my other past life) was in Manassas, Virginia at one time.

I read in the book that Richard Taylor's mother was Elizabeth Lee, a relative of General Robert E. Lee. I have dealt with several people with the name of Lee during my life so being related to them in the past was possible. For example, I have always felt that my friend Elizabeth Leslie was my mother in another lifetime. Please notice 'Lee' in her last name. Also, in my own mother's maiden name Gillespie see the word 'Lee'. One of my employers had the middle name 'Lee'. I noticed the name Elizabeth Lee on a street sign and often drove on 'Lee' Road down South. I used to live in Leon County (pronounced Lee) in Florida. I have been told that I resemble the actress Elizabeth Taylor, consequently, the name Taylor often comes to mind.

I was stunned to read in the book that the daughter-in-law of Richard Taylor had the same first and middle name of a lady who attended my church in South Carolina.

Taylor had sustained a leg injury during an indian skirmish. I too have leg trouble and do not walk well. I also read about something that was familiar in my life... Richard had danced with a lady named Mary. This normally would not seem extraordinary, but it seemed to correlate with my story ''Chance Encounter'' where Ralph had also danced with a lady named Mary who was my look-a-like.

The name Taylor kept appearing in my life during my visit to Michigan the summer of 1998. For example, while making a call in a phone booth, I noticed the name Taylor carved on a piece of metal. My mother and I went to make extra keys at a place called Taylor Key Shop. Also, I saw the name on a building called Richard Tailor's Shop. This shop must have dealt with clothes alterations because the word was spelled 'Tailor' instead of Taylor. What's also interesting is that our first apartment was located in Taylors, South Carolina.

All these clues from Spirit seemed to me to suggest that I was once Richard Taylor the father of President Zachary Taylor.

Reminder of Fred

On December 8, 1997, I awoke to a beautiful winter morning. Peering out of my window, I watched as the white fluffy snow blanketed the trees and the ground. It truly looked like a Christmas card that came alive. Since it was a lovely day to take a ride, that afternoon I drove to Southfield where I had to pick up surveys for a marketing assignment with Kelly Temporary Services. The office, located near Telegraph and Northwestern Highway, happened to be next to the new Star Theater--a place I had just spoken about visiting a week before. I decided to visit the theater first because it was so close and then later get the surveys.

As I drove down the Expressway, my desired exit was Northwestern Highway. As I approached the exit, I noticed it read Telegraph/Northwestern Highway. For some reason I kept driving, thinking there was another Northwestern exit up ahead. Instead, I drove about four more miles to get off at the next exit at Orchard Lake Road. I finally reached my destination about ten minutes later than expected.

As I walked into the Star Theater, an older man spoke through a megaphone and said "Enjoy your show." I replied that I was just passing through to see the theater that my friends expressed was so large and exquisite looking. The decorations were done in good taste and the building props

127

appeared authentic, which made me feel like I was standing in the middle of a movie set.

Upon leaving, I walked over to talk to the announcer who introduced himself as Fred. He explained that he was 71 years old and of Jewish descent. During our lengthy conversation, I noticed a few similarities in our lives. Both of us had a son named Mark, with the same initials. His daughter's name was Lisa and my niece's name is also Lisa. His son was a magician and I performed some magic as a clown. The most amazing fact was that we met on December 8, the exact day of my friend Fred's demise, five years ago. Fred was about the same age as this man at his time of passing, and he was also Jewish.

When I talked about visiting the Star Theater on Thanksgiving day, did a universal force or the spiritual realm give me that chance? Everything seemed to fall into place. Kelly Services gave me this assignment close to the time I wanted to visit the Star Theater and their office happened to be next to the theater, giving me the perfect opportunity to visit there. Did meeting another man named Fred happen by chance or was it just another way that Fred communicated with me, perhaps not wanting me to forget him? Fred said that he started working at 3:00 p.m. that day. If I had not taken the wrong exit and arrived ten minutes earlier, I might have missed him.

Fred Speaks Again

Fred, my former boss, and I were good friends. We met while performing with entertainers in a Variety Show. A few months later, he asked me to work at his office supply store in Roseville. I accepted the offer, working part-time as a store clerk for about a year.

Fred passed away on December 8, 1992. One year later at the end of November, I met another Fred at a singles' dance while sharing the same table. He was 55, good looking, with dark brown hair and eyes. He had very little gray hair so he looked much younger than his age. There was a striking resemblance to my deceased boss, who even at 70 years old looked much younger, with brown eyes and brown hair with a touch of gray.

We had talked on the phone several times before Christmas, but only went out to dinner once. As New Year's Eve drew nearer, Fred asked me to accompany him to a party given by a singles' club that held meetings at a Lutheran Church. The festivities of the evening would begin with a worship service, to be immediately followed by a party at the home of one of the members. I declined the invitation at first, because I wanted to spend the evening with my young son. After some reflection, I decided just to go to church in my own car and meet Fred in the lobby. It was a beautiful service highlighted by a melodious choir.

Afterward, we walked out together. As we stood in the parking lot, Fred embraced me saying, "I really hate to see you go--I wish you were going to the party." He said these words with such passion, making me feel that we had known each other for many years. In reality, I only knew him for about a month. That was the last time I saw him.

On the fourth anniversary of his transition, Fred Remer made his presence known yet another time. On this chilly December 8th, I had gone to the bank drive-through window. As I sat in my car, right in front of me a van bore the name Remer's Surgical Supply.

Did my deceased boss Fred bring this other Fred to me to give me a divine message and then disappear from my life? This seemed evident because he never asked me out again. I believe angels can come to us disguised as humans to bring messages from heaven. Was seeing the name Remer at the bank another communication from the spiritual world? Seeing this van on the exact same day of his passing seemed surreal.

Raccoon on Balcony and my cat Chloe

Chapter VIII

Mother Nature

Blessed By Nature

While married for nineteen years, we lived in two different houses in Michigan. After my divorce in 1994, I continued living in my second home four more years. Since 1998 to the present I have lived in six locations. It has been a pleasure being with nature at three of these residences that have served as a stepping stone for another spiritual journey.

In 2003, both of my parents passed away within three months of each other. I then decided to sell my Preston house and move to a condominium also located in Sterling Heights. My condo was located on the second floor at the very end of the complex right in front of the woods. I could also see a pond a short distance away from my balcony. For me, this was the nicest location in the complex.

It was fantastic being in the midst of nature. A couple of days after moving there, I noticed a storm had caused a crack in a tree that blocked part of my view. They soon cut down that tree so I could see the woods much better. Also it was amazing that another tree was bent over low enough allowing me have a nice view of the woods.

Every day it was such a joy to see several deer romping through the woods. One morning about 8:00 a.m., I awoke to see a large deer, then watched as an adorable fawn came out of the woods to the edge, near the lawn. The large doe (presumably its' mother) started to prance toward the baby. The fawn then followed it back into the woods. What a precious sight to behold! On another occasion while standing outside, I saw three deer walking through the woods. One stared at me -- I made a kiss sound, and it kept looking, perhaps hoping for some food.

At dusk, a family of raccoons would climb up the back wall of my condo and then onto my balcony. I thought of them as pets from Mother Nature and fed them regularly. My curious cat would sometimes join them on the balcony but luckily they never attacked her.

One afternoon after a shopping spree, I returned home to discover a raccoon was in the bedroom located near the woods. I watched it grab a cookie box and quickly leave. He had entered my bedroom through the doorwall off my balcony. Thus, a lesson was learned to never leave the doorwall unlocked when I go away.

My cat, Chloe, also seemed to love nature. On three separate occasions, she carried in two birds from the balcony and brought up a chipmunk from the woods. We were able to get the birds out okay, but the chipmunk had to be taken out by animal control.

Almost every night I was entertained by several winged creatures. It was fun to watch a woodpecker pecking on a nearby tree, bats flying from the woods, and fireflies adding a glow to the festivities. Also, at night while I laid in bed, an owl would vocalize "whoo". Maybe it was there to sing me a lullaby so I could drift into a deep sleep.

In the Fall, after the trees had shed their leaves, I would look out of my master bedroom window and see the pond glistening in the sunlight. To add to this beautiful scene, one or two swans would appear swimming with graceful ease.

In 2007, I moved to the Villas of Shelby, a retirement facility with a nice atmosphere and pleasant staff. I lived at the end of the first floor across from the woods.

At times, I would see ducks walking down the back path in front of the woods. One day as I gazed outside, a deer appeared standing close to my French doors. Another time there was a groundhog standing near my apartment.

The most exciting event happened when my daughter-in-law, Laurel, and I went outside one evening to see flying squirrels performing acrobatics from tree to tree. There are not many of these animals around, so we were lucky to experience them.

After one year of living at the Villas, I decided to move to Tallahassee, Florida where my son Marc and his wife Laurel were living while he was attending college there. Living in North Florida, about a hour from the Gulf of Mexico, was very scenic with rolling hills, lakes, palm trees, and exotic plants and flowers.

Every night I looked forward to seeing a couple of foxes wander in my backyard near the lovely tall trees. Often, we would leave cat food for them which they seemed to enjoy. However, they had competition occasionally when an opossum would eat some of the food. Once in a while, a raccoon would join the party.

My neighbor lady, Meghan, whose dwelling was attached to my townhouse noticed some holes dug on the side of our building. Thinking it could have been an animal, we hired a company to set traps in that area. Well, it turned out we had an armadillo in our midst. The company brought one trap into my house, and showed me this troublemaker, and mentioned that armadillos sometimes borough underground to make their homes. It was cute, but the company had to take this animal and drop it off in an open field.

We also welcomed a visit by a very tiny snake with colorful stripes, 1/2 inch in diameter. We found out that he was a Scarlet King snake. He must have slithered up the porch wall and under the door to enter the porch.

Our other visitors were little lizards. When I went out my front door, occasionally there would be these little lizards attached to the walls of my entrance way. They were harmless, but when I touched them, they would change colors to protect themselves. One day my cat carried one inside and dropped it on the floor. The lizard moved quickly, but the cat kept grabbing it until it was limp making it easier to take it outside.

Sometimes, while looking out of my living room window, I would see a bald eagle or hawk fly by. It was so relaxing to see them glide across the sky as if they did not have a care in the world. Also, how I loved watching a little rabbit hopping in the yard around dinner time.

We would walk by a retention pond located close to our house and sometimes see a family of geese that were on land or swimming in the pond. We noticed that the father would sometimes stay on land while the others went in the pond. He seemed to be on the lookout for any suspicious predator and then would slowly join his family. The little chicks were such darlings. Also, when going by the pond, it was fun to see a big turtle swim underwater.

Another adventure with nature came about when we visited St. Mark's Nature Preserve where we saw a family of wild boars walking across an open field. On that same day there was an alligator right next to the road. When we pulled over to get a better look, he opened his mouth extremely wide obviously threatened by our presence. We were certainly glad to be in a van safe and sound.

Visiting Wakulla Springs was nature at its finest. We toured the river on a boat while being engulfed with many birds, ducks, fish, alligators, turtles, and various insects. We were also fortunate to see Manatees,-- large mammals that sometimes swim underwater near the boat. With all the exotic trees and swampy areas it was obvious why this was the best choice to have filmed the Tarzan movies among others.

I believe that all the nature described above came to me from spirit so I could experience its' beauty firsthand. In my numerology chart it reveals I like Music, Nature and Solitude which happens to be my initials--MNS. I was truly blessed by nature.

Leaving Preston

In 1978 our family moved from Eastpointe, Michigan to Preston Drive in Sterling Heights. My husband and I divorced in 1994 but I stayed living in the house four more years with my sons. From 1998 to 1999, we resided in South Carolina and Grosse Pointe Woods, Michigan, before moving back to Preston in 2000 to 2003.

Between 1994 and 1997 we had a few unfortunate mishaps which made me speculate if it was time to move out of Sterling Heights for good. These were some difficulties we endured:

1. My son Michael and his carpenter friends had done a great job replacing the roof on the house. Unfortunately, when the large dumpster came to discard the old roof debris, my driveway became badly cracked. We explained the situation to the company who provided the dumpster, but they said they were not responsible for the damage. Consequently, we had to have a large part of the driveway replaced.

2. We had an issue with some mice making their home in the ceiling of our basement. These unwanted house guests would come up in the middle of the night and leave shredded pieces of paper in the living room. We also had a visit from a raccoon who came down our

chimney one night while we slept. Being afraid, he went into the front closet because the louver doors were slightly open. The next morning, we heard a noise in the closet. Upon opening the door, to our surprise, we saw a frightened raccoon. My son secured the door, and called animal control to remove the intruder.

3. Our yard had poor drainage which had always been a concern. Instead of the land sloping away from the house, it sloped toward the house so when it rained we would often have water in the basement. Also, in the late 1990's we noticed a crack in the basement wall.

4. In December of 1997, the city cut down the tree in front of my house, located near the street. Apparently, it had become diseased and had to be taken down. This made me very unhappy; and I remember thinking they might as well be cutting off my arm because it was so hurtful to see this tree gone.

5. Marc was involved in a car accident. The traffic was exceptionally heavy in this area because a nearby bridge was down. As he turned left from a business driveway, a car in the left hand lane hit him. Our car had considerable damage on the driver's side. He was taken to emergency, x-rayed, and released with no apparent injuries.

The ironic part of this was that only one week before, we had cancelled an already paid for insurance policy that covered collisions. Consequently, the repairs cost us over $5000. I honestly don't remember why I cancelled this policy, but I know it happened for a reason.

With all these unfortunate situations concerning the house and property it seemed as though it was time to move out of the house. Plus the fact that there were some unhappy memories here that I wanted to forget.

As for the car accident-- why was this bridge being repaired at the time we moved back to Sterling Heights? Why did the accident occur only one week after we cancelled the insurance policy? This seemed *to* reinforce the fact that we shouldn't have come back here to live. Also, this accident happened only about a quarter mile from my home. Because so many things had been a challenge, this seemed to be a divine calling, telling me to move out of this house.

The Dove and the Cat

One day while at work during the 1990's, a dove flew into our large warehouse door-- the only time in three years I've spent on the job that this had happened. It stayed in the warehouse a few hours before Harry, our service technician, could finally coax it out.

A few minutes had passed, when a cat wandered into a small door leading to my office. It stood in the vestibule for about three minutes; looked at me, then turned around and walked out. Why was the dove and cat there on my day in the office? I had only worked two days a week.

Doves seemed to be around me often. I would occasionally see them perched on the electrical wire between my house and garage. One day, while standing in my parents' driveway, I just happened to look up to see two doves on the television antenna. They also appeared in the parking lot at work quite often. As I drove home, It was a delight to see doves on the grass next to the road.

I believe doves are a sign of good luck and peace. Although they were not white, to me they still represent the Holy Spirit. Seeing a cat and dove on the same day could also be a message from two deceased loved ones checking up on me. I believe many times people that have transitioned who care for you can show up as animals, birds, or butterflies, etc.

The Spider and Flies

Upon moving back to Michigan from Florida, we had a wonderful housewarming/ birthday party with entertainment which included an Elvis impersonator, a clown and a dance routine performed by my greatnieces. Many friends and family helped celebrate my purchase of a foreclosed house and also my son Marc's 30th birthday.

We received many gifts among which was a beautiful orchid given to me by my friend Lynne. We decided to put the orchid plant next to the kitchen window. One day we noticed a big spider residing in the pot. I enjoyed watching him make huge webs and seeing him crawl inside the plant to hide. Also, what became my pet spider knew that we had many flies buzzing around the house which mainly flew in from the family room door. I'm sure he salivated often, hoping to catch a good meal.

At times I have had trouble keeping flies out of my house. While living at my Michigan condominium, I had an infestation of about fifty flies. Somehow, one got inside and found a way to survive. At first, I didn't think much of it because everyone has problems with flies every now and then. However, it became annoying when so many of them flew above my head making loud persistent buzzing sounds.

I began wondering what the real or spiritual reason was behind these two creatures. Spiritually, there was something good that came from something bad. Something bad was when the flies flew around me making loud buzzing sounds. Something good was realizing that I do much better with people who are quieter and move slower like the spider compared to people who are fast moving and noisy like the flies.

Spirit confirmed what was learned from this message a couple of days later. When getting out of the bathtub, I noticed a spider on the floor next to my foot. In the past few weeks, I stated, ''I seem to like quieter people who are reserved like myself. ''

Chapter IX

Messages

Magical Messages

As revealed in many of my experiences, paying close attention to details has given me clues bringing me life changing information. These clues allow me to see present and future events. One might consider this a gift from the Universe. Being diagnosed with Multiple Sclerosis, sitting in a scooter, and minimal walking each day has granted me time to notice these details. Many people are so busy with their lives that they just don't pay close attention to the world around them. These magical messages describes some of the service I do each day.

1. In 2008, while in Tallahassee, Florida I noticed a building that housed trucks that would be used to evacuate people in case of a hurricane. I also noticed signs that read evacuation routes. Seeing the word 'evacuation' in a spiritual way could mean that everyone might be taken off earth temporarily due to planetary changes, then brought back when safe to do so.

2. While driving in Florida, I noticed the word ''Meek'' on a billboard. In the Bible, Matthew 5:5, states ''Blessed are the meek, for they shall inherit the earth.''

3. Passed by a business in Florida that said "Higher Ground" on the side of the building. With all the devastation caused by earthquakes and hurricanes, floods and other disasters that we have, moving to higher ground is essential.

4. After my father passed away in 2003, it seemed like he left a message on my bedridden mother's pant leg. It said,' I love you'... it appeared like the letters were made from salt used to melt snow.

5. While driving in Florida the letters 'ET' were seen on a hill next to the highway. This could signify extraterrestrials.

6. Saw the word 'portal' on the back of a greeting card, and the word Stargate Street on my MS support group address list. Noticed lights flashing in my kitchen, on my son's bicycle and in the sky. Could these possibly be reminders of UFO'S ?

7. On a Luv Yu cookie box, I saw YU55 (55 was on the bottom of the box) which is the name of an asteroid.

8. As I looked on a bottle of La Tourangelle Artisan Oils-Toasted Sesame Oil- handcrafted in Japan, the words 'Japanese tsunami,' was seen on the label just after the March 11, 2011 tsunami in Japan.

9. Went to neurofeedback sessions to help my health condition. I watched the screen with a spaceship going through a tunnel while listening to beautiful music. Also, I saw the word wormhole. Could this also relate to space travel someday?

10. Almost every night I use a sleep aid called 'Rescue Remedy'. I have been seeing the word 'rescue' several times, which may relate to my having been saved/rescued from potentially harmful situations several times in my life.

11. While looking out of my living room window in Florida, the word 'EGO' was clearly visible on the grass next to my townhouse. The word EGO could mean to Edge God Out.

Shapes and Rainbows

Through the years, I have encountered some heart-warming and colorful experiences. Many shapes and rainbows have crossed my path leaving me with a refreshing sense of awe and feeling of importance on my journey as a lightworker. It's like these hearts that continually appear are a reminder that I am loved and will be taken care of by Source and the magnificent cosmos.

One Summer day while living in Florida, I went outside and noticed a large perfectly shaped heart in the grass. When I showed my friends and family, they agreed that it looked like a heart. Could this have been a mini crop circle with a message?

Hearts have appeared other times in my life. Two hearts appeared on my kitchen floor... when beet juice spilled forming a heart; and a rainbow heart, which probably came from a reflection of the cut glass window on my front door. Another time I noticed a heart on my face. In Michigan there was a heart shape on my driveway made from snow. I purchased a piece of red meat some time ago that was in the shape of a heart. There was a heart shape on my Tupperware lid.

Many times I have noticed 'XX's, 'V' or upside down V shapes appear around me. For example, one morning I awoke to see an upside down V on my arm. Another morning this shape appeared on my face. At a prayer partners' meeting, the cake had an upside down V design on it. One evening, when disposing my garbage outside, I noticed a cloud shaped like a V and another evening, there were stars in a V formation. An advertisement on television describing an upcoming show on Egypt, showed drawings on the buildings with several upside down Vs.

' XX' designs were in the lattice at the Palmetto Center at my temporary job assignment in South Carolina and on wallpaper at a model home during another assignment. My neighbor's house located in Warren, Michigan, has a lattice laying against the bricks.

Did these 'V' formations signify a pyramid, a bow of a ship and a teepee? A psychic spiritual minister had told me I lived in Egypt in a past life. I believe I was a Cherokee Indian at one time. When seeing the 'XX' shapes, it sparks a memory of the lattice at the Cafe Parisian on the Titanic and also 'XX' was on the furniture and decorations on the ship.

Another interesting phenomenon has been all the rainbows appearing in my townhome. For a few days, it was enchanting to see a rainbow appear on my hallway carpet, even though there wasn't a window nearby--this was a miracle. Rainbows have appeared on my kitchen walls regularly that were probably caused by reflections of suncatchers on my windows. Suncatchers were the physical, but the real or spiritual meaning was to see rainbows.

Never in my life have I seen a double rainbow until it appeared one day after a rainstorm in Florida. It really took my breath away while witnessing its beauty.

God puts storms into everyone's lives as we face trials and tribulations. Once we depend on him for guidance, then a rainbow will appear after the storm. Seeing the beauty of the rainbow and knowing the meaning of its colors, also helps you forget the storm you just went through.

Similar Names and Numbers

Many times messages come through that correspond to different times in our lives. They may be seen as addresses, street signs, building names, billboards, etc.

While driving down Gratiot Avenue in Michigan with my friend Ray Cook, we noticed a store named Cook's Lamps. Soon after, we saw a sign for Ray's Electric.

When I married in 1973, we lived on Melrose Street in Michigan. My father-in-law, a widower, was named Melchior, Mel for short, and his new wife was Rosemary.

Before moving to Greenville, South Carolina in 1998, my boyfriend and I went to his trailer in Marine City, Michigan. As we drove, we came across three interesting street signs. The names were Rose, Taylor, and Green in consecutive order. After seeing these signs, I moved to my first apartment in Taylors, South Carolina and my second apartment was in Greenville, South Carolina. My spiritual name is Rose. One can see how the names of these street signs correspond with the above references in my life.

When we first arrived in South Carolina from Michigan, we had to return a Ryder truck. As we drove down the main street, Wade Hampton Boulevard, we got lost and noticed familiar street names. I believe the real or spiritual reason behind this was to see Caldwell and Wedgewood Streets. Caldwell was the street where I grew up, and Wedgewood was a street located near my home in Sterling Heights.

My neighbors in Sterling Heights were Jan and Darryl--my neighbors at my apartment in Taylors, South Carolina were Jan and Darryl.

The numbers 4,7, and 9 often appear in my life. In May of 2003, I decided to move to a condominium... The asking price was $149,900 and the address numbers were 4799. The address of one of my apartments in South Carolina was 4990. My parents' address numbers were 4292. The building address where I worked had the numbers 1490. One of my address numbers was 17194 which also was my grandmother Christine's house at one time. My grandmother Julia's address had 194--see 194 in each of my grandmothers' addresses. My birthday is 10-7-1949 which has 17194. My parents' old telephone number was 673-1791.

My deceased ex-husband was only gone about a month when he made sure I didn't forget him. While living at the American House in Sterling Heights, Michigan during the summer of 2010, I went outside on my scooter one day and felt drawn to go across the parking lot. I soon came upon a truck with a spare tire at the back of the vehicle. I was stunned to see on its cover a smiley face and the words Chrysler, Sterling Heights. Also, number 19 was on the license plate. Mike was a big fan of smiley faces and had worked at Chrysler. We were married 19 years, 15 of those living in Sterling Heights.

When One Door Closes Another Opens

One beautiful summer day in Michigan, my son Michael, daughter-in-law, Theresa, and granddaughter, Jennifer and I were on our way out to go to a nearby bowling alley. After we walked out, my son suddenly realized that he had locked the keys in the house. The house and car keys were on the same keychain. We were quite concerned because we obviously didn't want to break a window or a door to reenter. It then dawned on me to call my roommate to get the house key from her. He knew where to find her because she was visiting her mother near where Michael's dad went to school. He returned with the key, which enabled him to get back into the house for both keys.

We then proceeded to go to the bowling alley and enjoyed watching Jennifer bowl. When we returned home, we discovered the family room door wide open. Being in a hurry, my son had left it open.

We have all heard the expression 'when one door closes, another door opens'. One example of this would be...If you lose your job (closed door) there is a good chance another job (open door) will soon become available to replace it.

Number 838

I have had a passion for numerology for the past few years, so I was spellbound when the number 838 kept showing up during the summer of 2010. It seemed like part of the reason was to remind me of my former husband Mike. If you add 8,3, 8 = 19, you get the number of years we were married. On the evening we drove back from his funeral, and pulled into the parking lot, the clock in the car read 8:38.

These numbers continue to appear in my life experiences. My townhouse address in Tallahassee, Florida was 1304 and my neighbor next to me was 1308. When I add 1,3,0,4=8 and notice 38 in my neighbor's address I get 838. My roommate said she was born at 8:38. On the label of one of my vitamin bottles is 838. My homeopathic remedy was 8381. The numbers 838 appeared on a package sent to me. In my numerology chart, my attitude number is 8 and my personality number is 38. Many times when I look at the clock it reads 8:38.

Often I have noticed the number 38 in someone's phone number. Also, the number 19 has been in my life in other ways besides the number of years married. I believe fate has brought these numbers to me to show I'm on the right path.

Numerology

To calculate Life Path and Attitude numbers, one only needs to add up the digits in one's birthdate. For example, I was born on October 7, 1949. By adding 10 for the month, 7 for the day, and 1+9+4+9 for the digits in the year, the total is 40. By separately adding up the digits of that sum, 4 + 0 equals a single digit answer, 4, which is my Life Path number.

To find the Attitude number, only add the month and day. Then add the digits of that sum until one gets a single digit answer. For example, with my birthday, October 7, add 10 + 7, which equals 17. That number is reduced by adding 1 and 7 to get the Attitude number of 8.

So what do these numbers mean? As an example, here are two numbers that my son Michael and I share in our numerology charts:

The Life Path 4 are down to earth and born teachers. Their brains tend to overthink--keeping a journal would help. They like to have a garden and love nature. The male 4, needs security and goes out of its way to help others. They really want to be a good provider. The female 4 is very responsible and often gets a job to help the family. The 4 vibration loves honesty and are very sincere. They prefer having friends who are quiet and dislike people who are loud. They love their home and get upset if it is not kept up. They need enough fun and relaxation in their lives to avoid depression.

The Attitude 8 tends to be outspoken. However, when expressing their opinion, they are tactful and speak in a kind manner trying not to bring hurt feelings. They tend to spend money a little too freely. Sometimes they dwell too much on the past and should live more in the present moment.

A New Heaven and Earth

Presently, our Earth is undergoing major changes as it moves into the higher dimensions. We have been seeing many significant earth changes, especially all the earthquakes, hurricanes, tornadoes, floods which seem to be part of this process.

Revelation: Chapter 21: verse 1, in the Bible says: 'Then I saw a new Heaven and a new Earth, for the first Heaven and the first Earth had passed away.' This could mean that our current Earth will separate gradually by God's power, be rejuvenated, and then become a new Earth. The new earth will vibrate very fast as it enters the 5th dimension.

It is possible that for 1,000 years the new earth will have a paradise atmosphere where its inhabitants will be free of disease and never die. The ones who remain on a negative path sustaining a lower vibration not following spiritual principles, are likely to be left behind on the current earth. These people will eventually get to the new 5th dimensional earth only when they are ready.

Recently, I received messages when I saw the word 'Paradise' on the cover of my calendar and on a picture that I purchased at a garage sale. It was surprising to see "This is Paradise I'm tellin ya" on the picture. The physical reason I bought the picture was because it featured my favorite mafia male movie star. The real or spiritual reason was to later notice the word Paradise.

157

In two different stores, I received fabric shopping bags that had a large picture of the earth on the front. Also within a couple of months, I saw a picture of the earth on several holistic magazines obtained from my health practitioner. Seeing these so close together seems to suggest that Paradise Earth is just beyond the horizon.

Another remarkable revelation occurred on September 3 and 4, 2013. During a television advertisement, they announced "The Big One", regarding a huge sale featured in the store. I heard it twice on September 3. I also said the words "The Big One" on Oct. 11 in regards to the size of a container needed for personal use. On September 4, I received more information that was uncanny.

1. My health center gave me a flyer for an 'Electro Interstitial Scan'.

2. The therapist at the health center put my feet on a machine that vibrated very fast.

3. When I phoned another therapist, she stated that she would be giving the scan on October 12. I found out later that this date was changed to October 26. Was the date of October 12 given to me for a reason?

4. The health center's address has the number 28755. If we add 2+8=10 and 7+5=12 and 5 for 5th dimension. Their business card had a picture of the earth and the word 'Universal.'

5. Noticed numbers 5764 on a package sent to me on Oct 8. Please see 5+7=12 and 6+4=10.

158

I have noticed a few other pictures of the earth around me through September 10. These included two spiritual guide magazines that just happened to be on my computer desk each donning an earth. I also noticed for the first time, a picture of earth on a bottle of a liquid supplement that I have had for three years...obviously I was meant to see this at this time.

To interpret these messages, my third eye saw in the initials of Electro Interstitial Scan, E I S which transposes to Earth Is Separating. When my feet vibrated very fast that showed me the new Earth will also vibrate very fast. The other therapist mentioned the date of October 12 which corresponds with the address of 28755 adding up to 10-12 or October 12 and the other 5 could mean 5th dimension. This is one way I interpret numbers. The business card showed the earth and the word Universal, all adding more pieces to an earth changing puzzle. As for the words "The Big One"... every time these words show up, there is a big noteworthy event that happens soon.

These messages seemed to relate to the new earth and the most powerful Category 4 Cyclone that India has ever seen. On October 12, 2013, with wind speeds up to 215 km per hour, Cyclone Phailin caused widespread damage affecting 500,000 people.

It might be possible that from October 12 (Columbus Day) on, we will witness a gradual shift of our consciousness preparing us to ascend to the 5th dimension on the new earth. After our ascension, we should notice a new level of infinite possibilities with the divine and experience instant healings, telepathic communication, teleporting, traveling much faster than usual, dome buildings, community living, and more.

159

Sensible Sayings

There are many sayings with special meanings that are important to follow. They consist of only a few words, are easy to remember, and can have a huge impact in our lives. I have noticed a big improvement in my daily life now that I follow these powerful sayings.

1. Put ourselves in somebody else's shoes. This helps us understand what they are going through.

2. Say Peace, Love, Joy and Harmony. Many times I say these words at the beginning of an argument with someone because it helps to diffuse unhappy thoughts.

3. Do release work. Say very loud "Whatever is causing (your health concern) to leave me now!" Repeat this several times with great emphasis.

4. There are two sides to every story. If someone complains about another person, we have to also listen to the other person's point of view.

5. Laughter. Many times when upset, I laugh about my troubles instead of resorting to tears. This makes me feel so much better!

160

6. Complete the sentence ''I am overjoyed and grateful now that...'' Write down what you want in your life that you don't have now as if it is already exists. It's important to stay focused to change your vibration, so it will come into your life.

7. ''Communicate with your soul. Your soul is linked with your mind. Your soul is involved with every decision you make in your physical life. It's very important to ask your soul to help your organs, and help your cells. For example, if your heart is a challenge, repeat several times I love the souls of my heart cells. Please help yourselves—excellent heart, happy healthy heart cells. Say Thank you and Hao (repeat 3 times each).'' Also repeat the number 3396815 for optimum wellness. For more information, you can purchase the book called "Power Healing" The Four Keys to Energizing Your Body, Mind & Spirit by Zhi Gang Sha.

8. We must always say the words 'at least' when dealing with difficult issues. For example, since my doctor diagnosed me with Multiple Sclerosis in 2004 it has been very difficult but, at least, I was fine when my children were growing up.

9. 11:11 When the time 11:11 appears on the clock the Universe is ready to receive your question or wish. The Universe will always have the answer 'yes'. For example, if you want a car... repeat for one minute at 11:11 a.m. and p.m., the words 'I can afford a car '... say this for several days. I read about a man who was granted his wish by following this method of speaking to the Universe.

10. Say the word 'HU', pronounced hue which is an ancient name for God. Say or sing HU out loud or silently about twenty minutes each day. Lately, one day I was in pain, and while chanting HU, the pain went away. Miracles have happened using this exercise.

11. Think of 5 things each week that you are grateful for. It is more beneficial to me when I repeat them out loud to hear my treasured blessings.

12. Always look at the clean floor rather than the dirty floor. This means that if you are upset with someone, your attention goes to their bad qualities (dirty floor) instead of focusing on their good qualities (clean floor). If you ponder this, you usually see that their good qualities outweigh the bad which takes your attention away from your anger.

Conclusion

Words cannot express the strong feeling residing within me to share the benefits of living each day seeing reality only through spirit. There, we discover messages and miracles in a wondrous atmosphere that allows us to experience a feeling of fulfillment in our lives. To accomplish most of this, we must always be grateful and give thanks everyday for our blessings. It's important to focus only on what we have, not what we don't have. For example, if your father passes away at a young age and your mother is still alive years later, be grateful that you still have her with you.

When we get upset, we have to immediately switch gears in our mind and think about or participate in a pleasant experience. For example, when babies cry, it's wise to give them a toy or a treat to divert their attention. Consequently, they stop crying and forget their troubles. The same is true with us--when we divert our attention with a nice thought or experience, we become happier.

As a very spiritual person, I do not believe in birth or death. Many scientists have said that all matter and energy in the Universe stays the same. The parts are just assembled into new combinations. Energy can't be born or die because it has no beginning or end, it just changes form. We, as soul, can reincarnate many times to learn spiritual lessons.

The Law of Karma states that if you have a conflict with someone in one lifetime you come back together in another lifetime to even the score.

It is important to note that life comes and goes in cycles. You will notice that some situations do repeat. For example, my first assignment while in South Carolina was located near my last job. I will never forget that before moving back to Michigan, I had parked within six feet from where I had parked on my first assignment, sixteen months earlier.

Seeing many events fall into place so perfectly, I believe that fate often plays a dominant role because things seem to be known ahead of time. Your astrology chart is also an accurate tool to see your future. My friend Robert Taylor once said when you go on vacation you make many stops along the way, but your final destination is where you are meant to be. Free will is occasionally involved and things can change, but it seems to be the exception rather than the rule.

When you raise your vibration, it will let you get clearer guidance from your higher self which is vibrating at a higher level. This is achieved by being in nature, meditation, laughing and singing, affirmations, volunteering, stating your name and saying 'I Love You' while looking in a mirror. You will have a better life if you engage in these practices.

My hope is that through 'Divine Reflections', the real meaning of hidden messages revealed in this book will inspire you and guide you to a magnificent spiritual journey that you will never forget.

Made in the USA
Charleston, SC
15 November 2014